More Titles by Cho Larson

Hearts for the Kingdom
Christ Revealed in the Hearts of His People

Treasures of the Kingdom
Christ Revealed in Gifts to His People

A Jewel of the Kingdom

Christ Revealed in the Spiritual Gift of Prophecy

Book III in the Kingdom Series

Cho Larson

WESTBOW
PRESS®
A DIVISION OF THOMAS NELSON
& ZONDERVAN

WestBow Press books may be ordered through booksellers or by contacting:

WestBow Press
A Division of Thomas Nelson & Zondervan
1663 Liberty Drive
Bloomington, IN 47403
www.westbowpress.com
1 (866) 928-1240

ISBN: 978-1-5127-4815-4 (sc)
ISBN: 978-1-5127-4816-1 (hc)
ISBN: 978-1-5127-4819-2 (e)

Library of Congress Control Number: 2016910523

Print information available on the last page.

WestBow Press rev. date: 7/5/2016

Dedicated to

The Bride

"The Spirit and the bride say, 'come.'"

Revelation 22:17

For the testimony of Jesus is the spirit of prophecy.

Revelation 19:10

Contents

Acknowledgments...xi

Womb of the Dawn...xiii

Introduction: Breaking the Silence.......................................xv

Part 1. The Essence of Prophecy 1

Chapter 1. Christ the Giver of Gifts.....................................3
    A. Jesus, of whom we testify 3
    B. Revelation...4
    C. New Testament Prophets? 6
    D. Authority to prophesy...7
        1. God's order of authority 8
        2. Authority of the Name..............................10
        3. Positional authority 13

Chapter 2. Christ the Focus 18
    A. What is the spiritual gift of prophecy? 18
    B. The foundation 19
    C. The point of change 20
    D. Who can prophesy?...22
    E. Where does a prophet prophesy? 22
    F. When does a prophet prophesy? 23
    G. Why is the spiritual gift of prophecy needed?..........24

Chapter 3. Christ the Center 29
    A. Fallibility in the use of this gift..........................30
    B. Misuse of this gift 30
    C. The experience of ministering in this gift 31
    D. False prophecies..32
    E. Getting personal feelings out of the way 33
    F. Self appointed prophets...................................... 34
    G. Don't mix up the gifts...35
    H. Personal prophecies 36

I. Don't avoid the hard part 37

J. Misconceptions..38

K. Is this just a messy gift?...............................40

L. Caution..41

M. Biblical Order 42

N. Consequences of Sin and Neglect................43

Part 2. Prophecy at Work in the Church 49

Chapter 1. Christ's Empowering Work 51

A. Ambassadors...51

B. Prophetesses 52

C. The Source.. 54

D. Qualifications: 55

Chapter 2. Christ's Living, Active Presence 60

A. Is prophecy for today?................................. 60

B. Be fearless..62

C. Exercising the gift..63

Chapter 3. Christ's Word Present in Prophecy............ 68

A. Encouragement to ask for this gift 68

B. Hazardous duty 69

C. The benefits...71

D. Receiving the spiritual gift of prophecy 74

E. Continue being filled 78

Chapter 4. Serving Together Strengthens the Gift............82

A: Prophecy works with other spiritual gifts 83

B. Team work..84

C. Leading the team 86

D. Better together 88

E. Jesus, the Giver of Gifts 88

Going Forward: The Call is Clear....................................93

Appendix 97

Notes, Quotes & Credits.. 99

Glossary 101

Acknowledgments

Gratitude overwhelms me as I read the words on the pages of this book regarding the Holy Spirit's powerful and impactful gift of prophecy. The spiritual gift of prophecy is a miraculous gift for the strengthening of the church, and the Spirit's strength is needed today more than ever. So many excellent resources have been placed at my fingertips to teach me, guide me, and center my attention upon Christ who is revealed in the ministries of this gift.

My wife, Susie, Christian friends, Bible study groups, godly Christian writers, family members, and many others have inspired me with words of encouragement. I owe a special "thank you" to my editor, Nikki Holland, who worked with me to make this book possible. The prayers and support of so many have been essential to bringing this book together.

It is as if clouds of witnesses, the apostles and prophets of old, have become my valued friends to encircle me and enlighten me with God's Word regarding this awesome gift. God has provided bountifully for every need along the way. Like a master builder who directs the construction for a house of worship, the Master's blueprint for His church in this day and age has unfolded in the words written on these pages.

My prayer is that the chapters of this book will pour out God's "autumn rain." May they be like the "dew of Hermon falling on Mount Zion." To all who have walked with me along on this pathway, many blessings in Christ Jesus, our Lord and Savior.

Cho Larson

Womb of the Dawn[1]

Oh Womb of the dawn,

What treasures do you guard in the folds of your garment?

Treasures of life abundant.

What unknown wonders do you conceal?

Wonders of incomparable, eternal value.

What lies in shadowy stillness awaiting the morn?

Dew of the morning to pour out on sons of righteousness.

What mysteries will unfold with the revelation of the Morning Star?

Mysteries like a fresh, new blossom, proclaiming the season of rebirth.

What undreamed masterpiece have you conceived to bring forth?

Creations of new life, unveiled at the first light of day.

What is secreted in the recesses of your hallowed sanctuary?

Whispers to be shouted with the advent of dawn.

What wonderful gifts do you hold in your vessels of gold?

Marvelous, life-giving gifts revealed to undeserving souls.

---

[1] Inspired by Psalm 110:3

Introduction

Breaking the Silence

"We have different gifts,
according to the grace given to each of us.
If your gift is prophesying,
then prophesy in accordance with your faith."
Romans 12:6

The ground beneath your feet is rumbling. The great seas are in turmoil. The mountains shudder and quake. The hills slide away and the earth trembles at the presence of the Lord, who desires to speak to His people, to pour out springs of Living Water from the Rock, Christ Jesus.[2] The desire of God's heart is to speak to His children, to restore souls, to strengthen our spirits, and to refresh our hearts.

Above all the means God uses to speak to disciples of Christ, His inspired Scriptures are written for us to hear the voice of God, to redeem us, to empower us, to lead us, and to guide us. The Holy Spirit, who proceeds from the Father and the Son, inspired the Holy Scriptures and now opens our ears to hear. He opens the eyes of our faith to see and our understanding to know the heart and desire of our Heavenly Father.

After Malachi's warning (proclaimed about 430 B.C.) went unheeded, God's people suffered through four hundred years of silence. This was a famine of hearing God's Word, as prophesied by the prophet Amos. How is this kind of famine possible when, in fact, the Jewish people were reading the Mosaic Law, teaching the Law, having lengthy discussions regarding the Law, and following the traditions of the Law during the four hundred years of drought? The answer should grieve our hearts. The people of Israel had God's Word written on scrolls. They deliberated on the Law and teachings from the Law in their synagogues

---

[2] Inspired by Psalm 114

with religious regularity. Boys were required to memorize the Law and the Prophets, ready to quote them at the spur of the moment. The Law was chiseled in stone and recorded on parchment scrolls with quill pens and carbon ink; but it was not in their hearts.

Christians today take great pride in having the whole canon of Scripture inside a bonded leather cover, with our names printed in gold foil. We have Bibles on the bookshelves at home. Bibles in our Sunday school classrooms with crayon marks in them. There are Bibles under the chairs in the sanctuary, Bibles in the church library, and Bibles in the public library. We have topical Bibles, Amplified Bibles, Bible commentaries, study Bibles, women's Bibles, Bibles for real men, and Bibles in more translations than you can count. But we are suffering a famine of silence.

Beyond a doubt, the canon of Scripture is complete. We must not add to it or take away from it. There is nothing written or spoken in the church today that can supersede the Holy Scriptures. We must always remember that the Bible is the inspired Word of God written down by the apostles and prophets as the certain Word of God for His people, the church. It is unquestionably complete.

But we are a fallible people, not unlike the children of Israel. Too often we interpret and teach the Scriptures with a prejudicial bent. Our teachings are subject to our personal preferences, our worldview, and our life experiences. Too often a pastor or evangelist with a strong and charismatic personality will teach to please the crowd or tickle the ears of the saints. Sermons are prepared to kowtow to constituencies with closely held belief systems. In short, we are vulnerable to our human failings and get off the narrow pathway too often and too easily.

God's desire is to speak to His people. But we, like the tribes of Israel who gathered at the foothills of Mount Sinai, tremble with fear when the whole truth of God's Word is proclaimed.

> "When the people saw the thunder and lightning and heard the trumpet and saw the mountain in smoke, they trembled with fear. They stayed at a distance and said to Moses, 'Speak to us yourself and we will listen. But do not have God speak to us or we will die'" (Exodus 20:18-19).

It is a weakness of human nature to more readily believe what pleases us, because the whole truth will certainly confront our sin. Too often, our natural tendency is to abandon the Spring of Living Water and dig our own wells (Jeremiah 2:13). We draw the cool water from our well, saying to the people, "Come drink of this water. It will refresh you." But there is no life in it.

Enter the spiritual gift of prophecy. This spiritual gift is given to the church as a balance, like a shepherd's staff to bring God's people together in unity, guiding us to the Good Shepherd's green pastures, and leading us beside still waters. Leading us to the refreshing Spring of Living Waters. When God desires to speak to the church in the moment, in the times we begin to stray, in the very instant our feet start to slip away, when we wander off course and become ensnared, God has provided a way for His church, His people, to be brought back on course.

When God's Word is misused to tear people down, ministries of the spiritual gift of prophecy will lift up the church. When divisiveness plants its evil seed in a local body of believers, the humble ministries of this spiritual gift will unite the church. True prophetic words offered in a gathering of believers will admonish, encourage, redirect, strengthen, guide, empower, and build up God's people like pillars in the temple that make the structure strong. "Wisdom has built her house; she has set up its seven pillars" (Proverbs 9:1).

Please join me in this study of the spiritual gift of prophecy, to learn the who, what, why, when, where, and how of the spiritual gift of prophecy. We will discuss the foundational history of prophecy in the church and the central focus of this jewel of a spiritual gift. The season is upon us when the church is called to embrace all the precious treasures our Lord Jesus, the Bridegroom, holds out to us in His nail-scarred hands. Do not reject this priceless jewel given to Christ's church for her own good, to beautify, to adorn, and to prepare His bride for His coming.

Our Prayer: *May our Lord Jesus Christ, by His resurrection power, by the power of the cross and by the powerful ministries of the Holy Spirit, guide and direct you through this study of the spiritual gift of prophecy.*

PART 1

The Essence of Prophecy

Point by point, we'll use Scripture to interpret Scripture to unfold the beauty of the Spiritual Gift of prophecy in this segment of the study. This gift is given by means of grace through the Holy Spirit who emanates from the Father and the Son. Our Lord Jesus Christ has called us to complete the work of the Great Commission by means of the Holy Spirit's gifting and empowering of His people, especially with the gift of prophecy. This prophetic gift is vital to a healthy, fully functioning church and is in harmony with God's established order within the church. The purpose of this spiritual gift is to strengthen the church, and it is most powerfully effective when ministered together with all spiritual gifts.

Christ is the center, the cornerstone, the focus, the truth, and light; He sent His Holy Spirit to instruct our hearts. He is the One who is revealed in the ministries of prophetic utterance, and it is by the Spirit of Jesus that New Testament prophets are given this precious treasure. Search with me to discover the source, the inspiration, the purpose, and the benefits of prophecy at work in Christian gatherings. Layer by layer, we will examine this gift and bring to light the working parts that benefit and strengthen God's people. As we survey this graceful gift, we will learn what it is and is not, the history of prophetic utterances, where to prophesy, when to prophesy, and how to prophesy. We'll also clear up common misconceptions about this spiritual gift, and answer the question about who qualifies to serve in this gift. It can be hazardous duty, but the benefits far outweigh the risks. In all of this, Jesus Christ and His very nature are revealed like light that pierces the darkness.

1

Christ the Giver of Gifts

A. Jesus, of whom we testify

Throughout Scripture we find numerous prophetic pronouncements given to the prophets by the Holy Spirit. These were God's decrees to His people, warnings of judgment against sin, and foretellings about Jesus Christ. The Old Testament prophecies are of critical importance, proving with complete accuracy all the events that led up to Jesus coming to earth: His miraculous conception by the Holy Spirit, His virgin birth, His life among us, His work, His death on a cruel Roman cross, His resurrection on the third day, His ascension to the right hand of the Father, and the coming of His Holy Spirit to establish His church with precious gifts. There is no doubt that prophecy is an integral part of Old Testament Scripture and that it points the way to salvation through the promised Messiah, Jesus Christ. We can be sure of this because all that the prophets wrote foretells of the coming Yeshua, our Lord and Savior.

The spiritual gift of prophecy is given to the New Testament church[3] by the Spirit of Jesus, and it should continue to be an integral part of the church. God uses those whom the Holy Spirit chooses to gift and empower to speak to His people; God warns them against sin, admonishes them, strengthens them, directs them, encourages them, blesses them, and teaches them. This gift continues to be available to God's people because God has not changed. We must receive all the

---

[3] The New Testament spiritual gift of prophecy could accurately be referred to as *congregational prophecy.*

good gifts God holds out to us in His mighty hand, because in the use of these treasures, we become empowered witnesses who lift Jesus Christ up, testifying of His power and might to save.

Proof Scripture: Genesis 3:15, Luke 1:68-80, Psalms 89:3, Isaiah 22:22, Daniel 2:35, Micah 5:2, 1 Corinthians 12:10, 1 Corinthians 13:10, 1 Corinthians 14:1, 1 Corinthians 14:3, 1 Corinthians 14:39, Malachi 3:6.

B. Revelation

The question Jesus asked His disciples, "Who do you say I am?" (Matthew 16:15), was not only for them but is for each one of us to answer. We cannot respond to this question by means of book learning alone, but we can respond to it from what is revealed by the Spirit in our heart of hearts. How did Peter know who Jesus was? In verse 17, Jesus says, "Blessed are you, Simon son of Jonah, for this was not revealed to you by man, but by my Father in heaven." We cannot know and *live* this truth simply by knowledge alone; it comes by revelation of the Holy Spirit of God.

This is the same revelation that is at the root of the spiritual gift of prophecy. The first step is revelation by the Holy Spirit, and this cannot come from any man —but from the holy words of God. How many times have you read a Scripture that you've often glanced at and suddenly a light comes on and you exclaim, "So that's what it means. I get it! I finally get it." This is revelation from the Spirit of Jesus and is part of the foundation of the spiritual gift of prophecy.

When you minister in the spiritual gift of prophecy, how can you be sure that what you proclaim is a true revelation from our Lord God? Listen to the prophet: "But if they had stood in my council, they would have proclaimed my words to my people and would have turned them from their evil ways and from their evil deeds" (Jeremiah 23:22). The psalmist opens our understanding of this: "I will praise the Lord, who counsels me; even at night my heart instructs me" (Psalm 16:7; see also Isaiah 11:2). When you are hanging out in the Lord's council chambers, you know what is on His heart, you know what grieves Him, and you know what brings Him joy. All this because you are dwelling in His holy presence.

Imagine that two girls who are already best friends embark upon a road trip from Seattle, Washington, to Miami, Florida. Hour upon hour, mile after mile, they talk and share the deepest thoughts of their hearts like never before. By the time they get to Billings, Montana, they can order lunch for each other. By the time they get to Kansas City, they can speak the other's thoughts. When they arrive in Miami, their words and conversations have become very familiar and respectfully intimate. This example gives insight into the word "council" and what it means to abide in God's council.

Instead, Christians have duct taped and patched together the veil separating the Holy of Holies, and we shudder to think of entering. Here is the challenge for all redeemed mortal beings: Our spirit is the part of us that can connect to, abide with, and hear the voice of the Holy Spirit speaking from within. Many times I know or have heard a word in my spirit, but my mind can't grasp hold of it. I see things that I cannot comprehend. I hear things and I can't take it in. This lack of awareness on the part of my human understanding is because there is some disconnect between my spirit and soul.[4] My soul (which includes my mind) is not fully subject to my spirit that has heard from the Holy Spirit. My flesh is not yet in agreement with my spirit and continues to mend the veil to keep me from dwelling in the councils of a Holy God.

Children first begin to learn with mental pictures. As their brains develop, they begin to think in words and sentences. It may be similar to hearing what God is speaking to His people as He prepares you to prophesy. As you begin in this ministry, you may well understand what the Spirit is saying through pictures you see with your spiritual eyes. In my experience, this means of revelation is certainly reliable.

From what I see in the Scriptures, God intends for the spiritual gift of prophecy to be common in the church today. Peter quoted Joel's prophecy: "And afterward, I will pour out my Spirit on all people. Your sons and daughters will prophesy, your old men will dream dreams,

---

[4] This disconnect isn't always something to overcome, as we see in 1 Corinthians 14:14. There are some spiritual things that the mind can never fully comprehend. (The mind is part of the soul.)

your young men will see visions" (Acts 2:17–18). Peter made clear that this Old Testament prophecy is being fulfilled in the church age. Seeing visions and dreams is at times the first step in ministering in the spiritual gift of prophecy. The next step is to understand and interpret the dream or vision so that it may be proclaimed according to the truth the Spirit intends. This understanding and interpretation can only come by the ministry of the Holy Spirit; therefore, the one who prophesies ought to wait until the Spirit compels him or her before giving the message to the congregation at an acceptable time.

When Pharaoh asked Joseph to interpret his dream, Joseph replied, "I cannot do it" (Genesis 41:16). Joseph continued, explaining to Pharaoh, "But God will give Pharaoh the answer he desires." We cannot understand or interpret dreams, visions, and revelations using formulas, methods, or systems of interpretation; this comes only by the Spirit of a Holy God. Scripture makes clear the source of understanding: "The man without the Spirit does not accept the things that come from the Spirit of God, for they are foolishness to him, and he cannot understand them, because they are spiritually discerned" (1 Corinthians 2:14). Simply speaking, the natural man, the flesh, cannot grasp hold of what is spiritual. But a new creation, a reborn spirit, is brought into fellowship and communion with a Holy and Righteous God.

> Our prayer: Lord, crush the rebellion of my flesh, restore my soul, draw me, all of me, into Your council chamber to have intimate conversation with You and to know the desire of Your heart so that it may be the desire of my heart. Open my ears to hear. Open my eyes to see. Open my understanding to know.

C. New Testament Prophets?

It is important at this point in our study to clearly distinguish between Old Testament prophets, the apostles, and those who minister in the spiritual gift of prophecy. Old Testament prophets and New Testament apostles spoke the very words of God with the authority of God. Their words must be obeyed and followed. By contrast, those who serve in the spiritual gift of prophecy receive a revelation from the Holy Spirit, and by the urging of the Spirit they must interpret what they see or hear into words they choose for the benefit of those who will hear. Their prophetic gift is for building up, strengthening, exposing sin, and admonishing the church. But they do not have authority requiring obedience except when they speak or quote the actual words of Scripture.[5]

A challenge in defining the spiritual gift of prophecy is that in the most general sense of the Hebrew and Greek words for *prophet*, there is a broad brush of meanings that change with context.[6], [7] Another challenge is that when prophecy is mentioned in Western culture, people automatically think of predicting the future—horoscopes, Nostradamus, and Zodiac birth signs.[8] Christians most often think of the Old Testament prophets: Isaiah, Jeremiah, Elijah, Elisha, and Ezekiel, just to name a few. The Apostle Paul's letter to the Corinthians made the point clear that all spiritual gifts are always important: "Since you are eager for gifts of the Spirit, try to excel in those that build up the church" (1 Corinthians 14:12). Does the church still need to be built up? Certainly, and all the spiritual gifts, including prophecy, are gifts that strengthen the church.

D. Authority to prophesy

Christ's authority vested in us as Christians is not limited to the spiritual gift of prophecy, but applies to all spiritual gifts and all ministries in the Holy Spirit. The next sections explore three means

---

[5] While we must obey the scriptural basis of a prophetic message, we are not required to obey the very words of someone ministering in the spiritual gift of prophecy. We see an example of this in the prophecy given to the Apostle Paul by Agabus regarding the dangers of his journey to Jerusalem. Paul ignored his warning and continued on toward Jerusalem. Paul ended up bound in chains, as prophesied, but this was all in God's perfect plan for Paul.

[6] See the appendix for Greek and Hebrew definitions.

[7] See the definition of *pastor* in the appendix.

[8] If you have questions regarding God's instruction on horoscopes, read Isaiah 47:13.

of authority: Christ's command, the Name of Christ, and authority that comes from our position in Christ. In all ministries and service of spiritual gifts, and especially the spiritual gift of prophecy, Christ is the Foundation, the Cornerstone, and the Capstone, as you will see.

1. God's order of authority

The authority to exercise the spiritual gift of prophecy comes by the command of our Lord Jesus Christ and is empowered in the believer by His Holy Spirit. We must submit ourselves and be under the authority of Christ, Who is Head of the church, His Holy Spirit, and godly shepherds who have been placed in the church to lead us. Only then can we effectively minister in this spiritual gift.

Any Christian who ministers and serves under the authority of Christ, having been gifted by the Holy Spirit, is blessed to minister in the prophetic gift of prophecy. And yet under Christ's authority, we are instructed to minister according to God's established order. What does God's order look like? How is it manifested in this spiritual gift?

First we see order in the trinity: Father is first, the Son is second, and the Holy Spirit is third. There is order in all of God's creation. God has also established an order of authority within the ministries of the Spirit. We must submit to serve under Christ's authority and to serve within God's established order as the following Scriptures teach us:

> "He was not far from the house when the centurion sent friends to say to him: 'Lord, don't trouble yourself, for I do not deserve to have you come under my roof. That is why I did not even consider myself worthy to come to you. But say the word, and my servant will be healed. For I myself am a man under authority, with soldiers under me. I tell this one, "Go," and he goes; and that one, "Come," and he comes. I say to my servant, "Do this," and he does it.' When Jesus heard this, he was amazed at him, and turning to the crowd following him, he said, 'I tell you, I have not found such great faith even in Israel.'" (Luke 7:7-9)

> *"No one takes [my life] from me, but I lay it down of my own accord. I have authority to lay it down and authority to take it up again. This command[9] I received from my Father." (John 10:18)*

> *"All authority in heaven and on earth has been given to me." (Matthew 28: 18)*

In Luke chapter ten we read that Jesus sent out seventy-two of His disciples. We see the results of the command of Jesus, giving them the authority of His Name to bless a home, heal the sick, open the doors to the Kingdom, and exercise authority over the power of the enemy. Jesus reported to them that, "I saw Satan fall like lightning from heaven." This is an example to help us understand the importance of being under the authority of our Lord Jesus Christ and His established order within the church as we minister. We too have been commanded by our Lord Jesus to do this same work. Because of His command and by His command, we have authority to minister; and by the empowering work of the Holy Spirit we minister and serve in His church with eternal results.

Our Lord has established an order of authority in His church, and we must continually submit, being under His authority. Christ is the Head and He has appointed pastors and elders over us to lead, guide, and provide loving discipline for the orderly functioning of spiritual gifts. "And God has placed in the church first of all apostles, second prophets, third teachers, then miracles, then gifts of healing, of helping, of guidance, and of different kinds of tongues" (1 Corinthians 12:28). Also, "So Christ himself gave the apostles, the prophets, the evangelists, the pastors and teachers" (Ephesians 4:11). In all God has created there is order. In the church, true to His nature, God has established order: "But everything should be done in a fitting and orderly way" (1 Corinthians 14:40). We could well paraphrase this: "Everything in the church should be done according to God's established order."

---

[9] We see in all of Scripture the close connection between God's command and conferred authority.

You may have experienced driving in a large, busy city like Phoenix, Seattle, Atlanta, or Miami. How long would it take you to get to work in the morning if there were no traffic laws, no traffic signs, no lines painted on the road, and no police to enforce the law? The imperatives of Scripture and the leadership and loving discipline of a pastor and elders are necessary to provide an authoritative covering for the orderly functioning of spiritual gifts within the church. Without this, our gatherings are thrown into chaos.

2. Authority of the Name

Here we will see the power and authority of the Name of Jesus the Christ, Son of the Living God, become evident.

> *"The seventy-two returned with joy and said, 'Lord, even the demons submit to us in your name.' He replied, 'I saw Satan fall like lightning from heaven. I have given you authority to trample on snakes and scorpions and to overcome all the power of the enemy; nothing will harm you.'" (Luke 10:17)*

This was not only applicable to the seventy-two at that moment in time but in our time as well. "You will tread on the lion and the cobra; you will trample the great lion and the serpent" (Psalms 91:13). This Scripture proclaims and prophesies man's dominion over God's creation to be reclaimed by man, that is, the second Adam, our Lord Jesus Christ. He did not reclaim this authority only for Himself but He also delegates it to all who are "in Him." "His rule will extend from sea to sea and from the River to the ends of the earth" (Zechariah 9:10). We see Jesus exercising this authority over nature: "What kind of man is this? Even the winds and the waves obey him!" (Matthew 8:27). This authority reaches into the church as well: "And God placed all things under his feet and appointed him to be head over everything for the church" (Ephesians 1:22). "The God of peace will soon crush Satan under your feet" (Romans 16:20). Note, *"Your feet."*

Early in the history of the Christian church, we see the Apostles exercising the authority of the name of Jesus. Peter and John come across a man crippled from birth. "Then Peter said, 'Silver and gold I do not have, but what I have I give you. In the name of Jesus Christ of Nazareth, walk'" (Acts 3:6). It is easy for us to dismiss this as the work of someone special — the Apostles. But we, like them, are called to minister Jesus' name. By this miracle we see positive proof that Jesus is alive and active, ministering to the lost, weak and helpless, and it proves beyond a doubt that His Name is still all-powerful and without limit. All who are called by His Holy Name are a part of the body of Christ, His church. We are all included in the royal priesthood of believers and are called to minister in the power and authority of His Name (1 Peter 2:9).

Even greater power of the Name is revealed to us. A man, who was likely a disciple of John the Baptist, was driving out demons in Jesus' name. Beyond a doubt, the Holy Spirit's wind will blow where He chooses, and He will use whom He will use. This man fully understood the power in the Name of Jesus and He ministered in this power to bring God's will to be done upon earth as it is in heaven.

> *"'Teacher,' said John, 'we saw a man driving out demons in your name and we told him to stop, because he was not one of us.'*
>
> *"'Do not stop him,' Jesus said. 'No one who does a miracle in my name can in the next moment say anything bad about me for whoever is not against us is for us.'" (Mark 9:38-40)*

In Acts 19:13-16, we see the other side of the coin and learn the importance of being within, or submitted to the "order of authority" that God has established. The sons of Sceva made a decision among themselves to use Jesus' name for their own work. They had no authority conferred upon them and they used Jesus' name in vain.

> *"Some Jews[10] who went around driving out evil spirits tried to invoke the name of the Lord Jesus over those who were demon-possessed. They would say, 'In the name of Jesus, whom Paul preaches, I command you to come out.' Seven sons of Sceva, a Jewish chief priest, were doing this. The evil spirit answered them, 'Jesus I know and Paul I know about, but who are you?' Then the man who had the evil spirit jumped on them and overpowered them all. He gave them such a beating that they ran out of the house naked and bleeding."*

It's worth repeating until we get it: The authority of the name of Jesus is given to us by God's command. In following His command, we submit ourselves under God's established order for the church and minister as Jesus' hand extended to those in need. When the seventy-two disciples were sent out to go before Jesus into the villages, Jesus did not physically go with each of them. He commanded them to go in the power and authority of His Name. We learn in Matthew 28:18 that this is also meant for us, His present day church:

> *"All authority in heaven and on earth has been given to me. Therefore go and make disciples of all nations, baptizing them in the name of the Father and of the Son and of the Holy Spirit, and teaching them to obey everything I have commanded you. And surely I will be with you always, to the very end of the age."*

Yes! "To the very end of the age." Right now!

Therefore we prophesy in the name of Jesus Christ, Son of the Living God, who created heaven and earth. We prophecy in the name of the resurrected Christ, who is the Lamb of God, the Lion of Judah, King of glory, the Lord Almighty.[11]

---

[10] ESV reads, "itinerant Jewish exorcists."
[11] We prophesy in the authority of His Name without claiming His authority for the words we choose.

3. Positional authority

We have authority to prophesy, by the power and anointing of the Holy Spirit, because of our position in Christ Jesus and His position of power and authority. What is Jesus' position and what is the significance of His position? Jesus, having completed His work of redemption, ascended into heaven and is seated at the right hand of God the Father. Taking His place at the Father's right hand, Jesus has authority over all God's creation. The Apostle Paul writes:

> *"I pray also that the eyes of your heart may be enlightened in order that you may know the hope to which he has called you, the riches of his glorious inheritance in the saints, and his incomparably great power for us who believe. That power is like the working of his mighty strength, which he exerted in Christ when he raised him from the dead and seated him at his right hand in the heavenly realms, far above all rule and authority, power and dominion, and every title that can be given, not only in the present age but also in the one to come. And God placed all things under his feet and appointed him to be head over everything for the church, which is his body, the fullness of him who fills everything in every way."* (Ephesians 1:18-23)[12]

How does Christ's position of authority at the right hand of the Father grant authority to the believer? We must understand that we who are in Christ partake in His authority conferred upon us, and we must submit ourselves under His authority. "And God raised us up with Christ and seated us with him in the heavenly realms in Christ Jesus, in order that in the coming ages he might show the incomparable riches of his grace, expressed in his kindness to us in Christ Jesus" (Ephesians 2:6-7). Our Lord Jesus ascended to the right hand of the Father, a position of power and authority over all God's creation. We who are saved by grace through faith are baptized into Christ and

---

[12] Also read: 1 Peter 3:22, Psalms 110:1, 1 Corinthians 15:25.

become a part of His body. We are in Christ and our Lord Jesus Christ is at the right hand of the Father. Can you see it? When we are in Christ and a part of His body, He will use us to minister His saving grace. This is similar to the way our brain rules over our hands, feet, mouths, and the rest of our bodies.

This is God's order of authority:

First, "One God and Father of all, who is over all and through all and in all" (Ephesians 4:6).

Second, Christ Jesus is in the Father and seated in His position of power and authority. "Don't you believe that I am in the Father, and that the Father is in me?" (John 14:10).

Third, the Holy Spirit is sent by the Father and the Son to indwell us. "Do you not know that your bodies are temples of the Holy Spirit, who is in you, whom you have received from God" (1 Corinthians 6:19).

Fourth, we are in Christ. "Christ in you, the hope of glory" (Colossians 1:27).

Finally, we come under the authority of Christ. "Then Jesus came to them and said, 'All authority in heaven and on earth has been given to me'" (Matthew 28:18). Because we are under His authority, Jesus said, "Therefore go" (Matthew 28:19).

We are now **His hands.** YES! His very hands extended to minister life to all who will come to receive of our Lord Jesus Christ.[13]

This is the purpose of His authority granted to us in His Name: "For we are God's workmanship, created in Christ Jesus to do good works, which God prepared in advance for us to do" (Ephesians 2:10). Before you were born, God knew you. He planned the course of your life, your natural gifts, the spiritual gifts He would give you and He prepared a work for you to accomplish as your part of His body.[14] The Holy Spirit empowers you to accomplish all that God has begun in you for His honor and glory and He has equipped you to do battle with weapons that have "divine power to destroy strongholds."

Jesus Christ, the Word, is the center, the focus, and the foundation of all prophetic ministries. The Spirit of Jesus is the source of every

---

[13] This is being a living sacrifice, Romans 12:1.

[14] Too many have chosen not to follow His plan. Yet it is never too late to begin.

word spoken by means of the spiritual gift of prophecy. Those who the Spirit gifts will minister in His name, by His command, under the authority of Jesus Christ, and within God's established order. Now hold out your hand. Think of your hand as being "in Christ." Completely enveloped in the hand of our Lord Jesus. When you extend your hand "in Christ" to those in need, your hand is the hand of Christ. This is important because without your hand being in His, your work and service are done apart from His authority.

Now hold a bright flashlight up to your fingers. What do you see from inside your hand? Red! Think of this as the empowering and gifting work of the Holy Spirit who dwells within you. Now when you extend your hand to do the work of the church, your hand is "in Christ" like putting your hand in a glove, and then empowered in the Holy Spirit to minister in all that you are called to do. But, of course, it's not only about our hands, but all of us, our whole being.

Your Journey Journal

Chapter 1: Christ the Giver of Gifts

A.   What is the purpose, the object of the spiritual gift of prophecy?

B.   Who is Jesus of whom we testify? Why is the answer to this question so important?

C.   By what authority does someone minister in the spiritual gift of prophecy?

Your Journal Notes:

2

Christ the Focus

When the running back steps out of bounds before catching the ball in the end zone, it's no goal. When the soccer player kicks the ball out of bounds, the opposing team gets to throw the ball in. When the baseball team's home run hitter misses the third base plate on the way to home plate, he can be tagged out. In a similar way, when ministering in the spiritual gift of prophecy, when Christ is not the central focus of our message, we go out of bounds, so to speak.

To stay in bounds, it is vital that we know what this spiritual gift is, how it came to be what it is, who is called to minister in the spiritual gift of prophecy and the who, when, and where of prophecy. In addition, it is important that Christians understand why this gift is given to the church.

A. What is the spiritual gift of prophecy?

Definition: Proclaiming to a gathering of the church what the Holy Spirit has revealed or whispered into your soul and spirit, often spontaneously.[15]

An example of simple prophecy may be this: while you are praying for a friend, a truth comes to mind (inspired by and proven in Scripture)

---

[15] This definition does not apply to those who minister in the office of prophet, but only to the spiritual gift. The definition of prophecy ministered within the office is: 1) to foretell, i.e. give a message from God, whether with reference to the past, the present or the future; 2) to foretell, i.e. to tell something, which cannot be known by natural means.

and you are compelled to share this truth with them. When you proclaim this message to them, this is a form of prophecy[16] and a good way to begin exercising this gift. Be encouraged to allow the spiritual gift of prophecy to mature beyond this level. But remember, the typical use of this spiritual gift is in a gathering of believers. It can be a Bible-study group, a get-together of Christian friends, a prayer gathering, etc. This spiritual gift will be further defined as we continue.

B. The foundation

The spiritual gift of prophecy is included in what Bible scholars classify as utterance gifts, i.e. voiced ministries of the Spirit. And prophecy is the most desirable of these spiritual gifts (1 Corinthians 14:1). This gift simply consists of receiving a revelation or message from God and speaking that revelation or message to a gathering of the church. Typically, those who minister in this gift spontaneously receive God's message, by the Holy Spirit, with such clarity and assurance that he or she is compelled by the Spirit to speak to those assembled at an appropriate time. This is a gift the Apostle Paul encourages **all** believers to be eager for. Even Moses saw the day ahead of him when prophecy could be common among God's people. "I wish that all the Lord's people were prophets and that the Lord would put his Spirit on them!" (Numbers 11:29).

The foundational purpose of prophecy is to build up, to comfort, and to encourage fellow believers (see 1 Corinthians 14:3). All Scripture regarding the gift of prophecy, when taken together, reflects the expectation that this should be a widespread gift among the priesthood of believers. Please understand that among New Testament believers, the principle use of this gift is not primarily to foretell future events (Agabus, in Acts 11:28 and 21:10, gives us an example of an exception). "For the essence of prophecy is to give a clear witness for Jesus" (Revelation 19:10 NLT). This Scripture is key to our understanding of

---

[16] We must not limit prophecy to this level, but we should be eager for all ministries in prophetic gifts.

the spiritual gift of prophecy. It is important to repeat this truth. The spiritual gift of prophecy being ministered in a gathering of believers is a witness, a positive proof, of the saving power of our Lord Jesus presently at work among His people.

The spiritual gift of prophecy is a key part of a cycle of ministry perpetuated by the Holy Spirit.[17]

Proof Scripture: Romans 12:6, 1 Corinthians 14:31, 39.

C. The point of change

Is the spiritual gift of prophecy the same as Old Testament prophecy? Prophecy and the nature of prophecies has clearly changed. No one today can claim to speak with the authority of Scripture, nor can they claim the same authority of the Old Testament Prophets and the Apostles who wrote the New Testament. The Scriptures give us a clear

---

[17] The more we step into this cycle, the greater our capacity will be to serve and minister within this cycle.

demarcation to signal the change in prophecy. "For all the Prophets and the Law prophesied until John" (Matthew 11:13). After John the Baptist, prophecy changed from foretelling Christ[18] to revealing Christ.[19]

In the use of the spiritual gift of prophecy, the Christian is not to be considered infallible, and must submit to evaluation. Those who hear, especially those in authority, must test the prophet or prophetess's words to see if they are true in whole or in part. Scripture is the standard, the plumb line, for testing every prophetic utterance (Isaiah 8:20, 1 Corinthians 14:29). Clearly the prophetic gift is for the purpose of revealing the mysteries of the cross of Jesus Christ, the resurrected and ascended Jesus Christ, and Christ the returning Bridegroom, for the strengthening, encouragement, and comfort of believers. This is what we see the Apostle John doing in the book of Revelation. Please understand that the Apostle John's words were written with divine authority of Scripture because John was commanded to "write what you see" (Revelation 1:11). For those who minister this prophetic gift in gatherings of the church today, the *general content* of the messages are spoken by revelation from the Holy Spirit but they do not carry the weight of Apostolic authority.

Today, those who minister in this gift must do so by the Holy Spirit's inspiration for the general content of their message. We must choose our words and manner of speaking by the Holy Spirit's leading and under Christ's authority. This is an awesome responsibility, but at the same time, we must not avoid prophesying for fear of making a mistake. We must submit to the examination of the church, but we are no longer required to be infallible (1 Corinthians 14:32).

---

[18] "I foretold the former things long ago, my mouth announced them and I made them known" (Isaiah 48:3). In fact, God is the only one who knows the future. He speaks through His chosen prophets who are His spokespeople. He revealed and continues to reveal Christ through His chosen prophets who are His spokespeople. Some Bible scholars contend that Jesus was the last of the prophets. Even a quick read of Paul's letters to the churches clearly reveals that prophets are given to the church in this age. The truth is that Jesus Christ was and is the center, the focus, the reason for all prophecy. And our Yeshua HaMashiach is the first and last, the greatest of all prophets.

[19] The spiritual gift of prophecy may include messages to the church regarding Christ's second coming. Typically, these messages will focus on revealing Christ to His people to prepare them as His bride.

D. Who can prophesy?

A prophet or prophetess is a person who receives revelation or a message from the Holy Spirit and proclaims God's message or revelation of Jesus Christ and the cross of Christ to a gathering of believers. We need to imprint this Scripture in our memories and meditate on it so we can clearly understand its meaning: "For the essence of prophecy is to give a clear witness for Jesus" (Revelations 19:10 TLB). In the New Testament church, one who is given a prophetic gift will speak what God desires to communicate to His people, revealing the heart of God in the present moment and opening a believer's understanding to the teaching and prophecies of Scripture regarding the mysteries of our Lord Jesus Christ and His saving grace.

E. Where does a prophet prophesy?

Typically, prophecies are to be publicly proclaimed. After all, what good is a revelation or message from the Lord if it is hidden under a bowl (Luke 11:33)? God's messages may be ministered in pantomime or by illustration as we see in Ezekiel chapter 4 and 5:1-4 and again in Acts 21:10-11. Prophecies may be written as we see in Jeremiah 45:1. Prophetic writing may come in different forms. It can be a letter, a note, prose, a poem, or an e-mail, etc. Prophecies may also be written in a book, as we see in Jeremiah 51:60. There are exceptions. When the Spirit gives a prophetic dream or message that is only personally significant, one may choose not to share it, but that is atypical. A guiding principle is that after we prophesy, we must submit to the examination of the church to hold us accountable for our words.[20]

Proof Scripture: 1 Corinthians 14:12, 1 John 4:1.

---

[20] Pastors and elders should not require that all prophetic messages be preapproved before they are presented to the church.

F. When does a prophet prophesy?

It would be difficult or even impossible to list all of the possibilities for when we might prophesy. One challenge we face in answering this question comes from our rights-based culture. In America today, we believe that we have a right to do what we think is right, when we want to do it. In the Kingdom Culture, in a gathering of believers, we do not have the right to do as we wish, when we wish. We must be under authority. We must be in submission to the guidance, leadership, and authority of pastors and elders.[21] Whenever you have this "covering," it is a good time to prophesy. The leadership may have guidelines as to a time that delivering a prophecy is appropriate. If we do not submit to the authority of our pastors and elders, who are under the authority of Christ, we are in grave danger of moving into false prophecies. But this doesn't mean you can only prophesy when they are within earshot, watching what you do and say.

Often, when Scripture is read, taught, and preached, the Holy Spirit will breathe into our spirit a revelation of truth or a word of encouragement, admonishment, or enlightenment. If the leadership considers it appropriate, they will allow those who are urged by the Holy Spirit to speak to those who are gathered. A prophetic word may come during a time of prayer and may then be shared at a suitable time. During a Bible study, the Lord may whisper a truth to someone serving in this gift for the strengthening of your brothers and sisters and at His urging may be shared with your group.[22]

We are not compelled or commanded to mirror or imitate the practices of the first century church, but we can learn from them. In the book *Preaching for the Church* I learned the following:

---

[21] Titus 2:15, 1 Thessalonians 5:12, 1 Timothy 5:17, Hebrews 13:17. This is a major countercultural concept, but in fact the church is and must stand by God's Word in contrast to our culture, otherwise we have no foundation to stand on.

[22] Remember that giving a prophetic message is not the same as sharing your own thoughts, knowledge, experience, insights, or opinions regarding Scripture or teaching.

"Early Christians had the practice of breaking out, after one of those [Scripture] readings, into conversation which included comments or explanations, thanksgivings and exhortation (1 Corinthians 14:26). Such conversations were called a homilia. Over the years leaders of worship began to incorporate what was expected to take place in such a conversation into a message by a preacher, a one-man homilia — and thus was born the science and art of "homiletics."[23]

But it's useful to remember that early church preaching represented an act in which all the worshipers took part.

I feel as if this gives me a snapshot into an early Christian gathering where believers would read the Scripture or letters from the apostles and then ask questions, comment, receive teaching, give a prophecy, hear a message in tongues with interpretation, offer a thanksgiving, sing a hymn or song, sing a new song in the spirit, or share an exhortation from the Lord. Look at how open such a worship service would be, leaving room for the gifts of the Spirit to be manifested through God's people.

G. Why is the spiritual gift of prophecy needed?

While reading and meditating on 1 Corinthians, a relevant verse jumped out at me:

"But God chose the foolish things of the world to shame the wise; God chose the weak things of the world to shame the strong. He chose the lowly things of this world and the despised things — and the things that are not — to nullify the things that are, so that no one may boast before him." (1 Corinthians 1:27-29)

---

[23] R. R. Caemmerer. *Preaching for the Church*, pg 56.

If every word spoken in church is prepared using thoroughly schooled "sciences and arts of homiletics" and learned doctrines, are we truly hearing all God has to say to us? Is it possible that our Lord God wants us to understand that education, training, schooling, degrees in theology, and doctorates of divinity are excellent; but so that you may not boast He will also choose to speak through the weak, the despised, and the lowly among you as well (2 Corinthians 12:9)?

In the exercise of the spiritual gift of prophecy, we see that it can appear to be somewhat subjective, i.e. subject to the experiences, training, worldview, personality and upbringing of the speaker. Because of the way New Testament or congregational prophecies are given by the Holy Spirit as an oracle,[24] the prophet, with the Spirit's help, chooses the words that translate the revelation to the congregation. In choosing our words, we must remember what Peter writes: "If anyone speaks, he should do it as one speaking the very words of God" (1 Peter 4:11). We must do our best to avoid slanting the message with our own thoughts and opinions, and then we must submit to the examination of other Christians. Because of our fallibility, when a prophet or prophetess receives a revelation, it is not good to say, "Thus saith the Lord." It would be better to say, "I believe the Lord has revealed this in my spirit. Please let me know if this is correct, or if any part of it is erroneous."

The purpose of the spiritual gift of prophecy, and all other manifestations of the Holy Spirit in a congregation, is to offer real, tangible evidence of the Spirit's continued, living, and active presence where God's people are gathered to hear and minister the Word. This gift is proof positive that God is present with us, ministering to us and through us for the honor of His holy name. Historian James Thomson Shotwell writes of the early church:

> *"To them the evidences of Christ's continued presence*
> *were of utmost importance, for they were the best proof to*

---

[24] The definition of an oracle is: a brief utterance, a divine oracle (doubtless because oracles were generally brief) and in the NT, the words or utterances of God. This definition clearly fits the pattern for ministering in the spiritual gift of prophecy to the congregation.

> *the Jews that Jesus was the Messiah. One sure sign of the*
> *Messianic advent was to be a common enjoyment of the gift*
> *of prophecy."*[25]

The spontaneous expressions of the gift of prophecy are spoken by revelation of the Spirit of Grace for the purpose of building up, encouraging, correcting, and edifying God's people who are called the church. Prophetic words spoken in a gathering of believers are a part of a dynamic, Spirit-perpetuated cycle of ministry that is an enduring part of the New Testament church. The spiritual gift of prophecy is needed today as continuing evidence of the Living God's presence — evidence that He is not just present as an icon hanging on the wall, or a cross at the front of the church, or in silver ornaments of worship, but living and actively at work among His people. The ministries of the spiritual gift of prophecy are evidence that as God's ministers speak the whole truth of the Gospel, the truth is received, believed, and changing hearts and minds for all eternity.

---

[25] J. T. Shotwell. *A Study in the History of the Eucharist*, pg 10.

Your Journey Journal

Chapter 2: Christ the Focus

A. What is the source of all ministries in the spiritual gift of prophecy?

B. What is the difference between Old Testament prophecy and ministries of the spiritual gift of prophecy?

C. Who can prophesy? Where and when do they minister in the spiritual gift of prophecy?

Your Journal Notes:

3

Christ the Center

God, whom we serve, is awesome in every way. It seems that He takes enormous risks when entrusting His work in the earth to fallible, weak, and sinful people. To my way of thinking, there is nothing we can do that He couldn't do better without us, but God chooses use "cracked pots."[26] Because we are imperfect people, we tend to use God's good gifts to elevate ourselves. In our human weakness, we tend to push ourselves to the front and give Jesus a back seat. We must be aware of these pitfalls so we can avoid them.

Even when God's people are not faithful, when we trip up and fall down in the work God calls us to do, He is faithful to accomplish His purpose and plan through us. In our human way of thinking we try to make the ministries of spiritual gifts into ecstatic experiences. We attempt to use the gift to please our friends or to make ourselves important. Apart from the Spirit's gifting touch, we appoint ourselves as prophets. We attempt to assert our control over the gift or just outright forbid the ministries of the spiritual gift of prophecy because it's just too messy to deal with. Too often we try to use the gift apart from God's established order and create chaos and confusion. We must rise above our fallible human nature to minister and serve according to the Spirit of Truth.

---

[26] Term used by Patsy Clairmont, author of *God Uses Cracked Pots.*

A. Fallibility in the use of this gift

Much of the misunderstanding regarding the spiritual gift of prophecy is because of our human nature. We all want to know what the future holds for us. We want to know that the girl we marry will be our wife for the next sixty years and we'll have three fine children, two boys and one girl, and that they will grow up to be Olympic gold medalists, a doctor, and a scientist and give us ten grandchildren to spoil. This desire drives many of us to read a horoscope or break open a fortune cookie. But in the ministries of the spiritual gift of prophecy, we must only follow the leading of the Holy Spirit.

B. Misuse of this gift

The spiritual gift of prophecy typically does not offer a view of our personal future. This Scripture provides a good perspective: "Sow your seed in the morning and at evening let not your hands be idle, for you do not know which will succeed, whether this or that, or whether both will do equally well" (Ecclesiastes 11:6). We just don't know. Most often, we are not meant to know, and the ministries of prophetic gifts rarely fill this void.[27] Instead we are called to entrust our future into God's hands and to walk by faith and not by sight (2 Corinthians 5:7). Abram was sent to "the land I will show you" (Genesis 12:1). He was given a command, and then he got his marching orders one day at a time. He received a general picture of God's call but not the details before he packed up his tent to embark on his journey.

There are many warnings against the misuse of prophecy, false prophecies, and self-inspired prophecies. It is important to know about these warnings and to see what prophecy is *not* intended to be. Giving a false prophecy may be likened to offering up "unholy fire" (Numbers 3:4)

---

[27] Many of us have heard stories of people who were made aware of future events in their lives and the lives of loved ones. Typically, God's purpose in this is to call us to pray and intercede on their behalf. But this is not the most common function of the spiritual gift of prophecy.

The problems with prophecy did not begin with the foundation of the Christian Church. Difficulties, misuse, abuse, and deception have been rampant among seers and prophets from the beginning. Ezekiel accused false prophets of his day: "Her prophets whitewash these deeds for them by false visions and lying divinations. They say, 'This is what the Sovereign Lord says' — when the Lord has not spoken" (Ezekiel 22:28).

God's prophet clearly and at great length confronts the false prophets, calling them "lying prophets" in Jeremiah 23:9-40. God promises the end result of their lies in v. 40 when He says, "I will bring upon you everlasting disgrace." When prophets, preachers, pastors, evangelists, and teachers tell people only what they want to hear, the end result is "shame that will not be forgotten." There are more than enough modern day examples of abuse with unchecked "personal prophecies." Misuse of this precious gift of the Holy Spirit, whether by intent or ignorance, will bring disgrace and shame upon any and all that exploit it.

C. The experience of ministering in this gift

We must also consider that giving a prophecy is not a super-spiritual or ecstatic "experience." When we make prophecy into something more than it is, we run the risk of becoming experientially addicted and we will be constantly pursuing the latest so-called prophet or prophetic message as if our entire spirituality depended upon it. Ministering in spiritual gifts must never be sensationalized. We must be aware of the common error of wanting, even demanding, the extraordinary and the exceptional to be frequent and routine. This causes false expectations and people will go home from a church service where no spontaneous prophetic message was given, no tongues and interpretations were ministered, no words of knowledge, no healing, no spontaneous spiritual song was offered, and they feel as if they didn't get their money's worth. They feel let down, and then they're off to whatever church will offer them the latest "fix."

D. False prophecies

We must also be aware of false prophecies. False, lying prophecies grieved God's true messenger, earning Jeremiah the moniker "the weeping prophet." He wrote, "My heart is broken within me; all my bones tremble. I am like a drunken man, like a man overcome by wine, because of the Lord and his holy words" (Jeremiah 23:9). The land of the tribes of Israel and Judah, God's Promised Land, was full of adulterers, and the land suffered for it. The priests and prophets were telling the people, in spite of their sins, that all was well. Verse 17, "They keep saying to those who despise me, 'The Lord says: You will have peace.'" They were declaring peace and safety while the people worshipped other gods in the foothills. Even worse, the priests and prophets were misleading the people, guiding them deeper into sin, leading them into disregarding God's commands and precepts. They dealt with the people unjustly by declaring blessings upon unrepentant sinners and filling them with false hopes. Verse 15 is a clear rebuke to false prophets. "Therefore, this is what the Lord Almighty says concerning the prophets: 'I will make them eat bitter food and drink poisoned water, because from the prophets of Jerusalem ungodliness has spread throughout the land.'"

In contrast to so many false prophets, Jesus taught the crowds that gathered around Him, speaking with uncommon authority, using words He heard the Father speak and not the words of other men. God showed Jeremiah a great failing among the prophets of his day. "'Therefore,' declares the Lord, 'I am against the prophets who steal from one another words supposedly from me'" (Jeremiah 23:30). They were stealing sermons and messages from each other and saying "the Lord declares" as if the Lord had spoken directly to them. Today we call this plagiarizing. Why would they steal another priest's or prophet's words? Because God was far away from these lying prophets and the only thing they could hear was the ring of another man's words in their ears. Their messages were stale and lifeless.

Today we see a similar practice among some pastors, preachers, evangelists, and teachers. They declare to the people, "God will bless you." Without hearing from the Lord, they quote Scripture out of context and tell the people, "God will give you good health and give you thirty, sixty, or even a hundred times return for your generous gift to my ministry." The shepherds of today fatten themselves as they prey on the people, proclaiming false words and empty promises that are not from God.[28]

Clearly, prophetic messages do not originate in our imaginations, impressions, intuition, or common dreams. Prophecy's purpose is not to please the ears of those who hear it. True prophecy typically does not serve to help us make personal decisions such as who to marry, where to go to school, what car to buy. New Testament congregational prophecy is **not** some kind of crystal ball to tell us about our personal future.[29] Faithful prophecy does not have its origin in the will or mind of a man or woman. Prophetic messages are not extra-biblical. Prophetic words cannot be borrowed or plagiarized from other men or women. Prophetic utterances must come only from what God reveals or speaks into our spirit, and all to the glory of Jesus Christ — before the godly and godless alike. Anything less than this is an offense to the Spirit of Jesus and comes with consequences, disgrace, and shame. It is like an unholy fire.

E. Getting personal feelings out of the way

Ken Blue writes about personal feelings in his book *Authority to Heal.*

> *"Some time ago, my aunt discovered she had cancer. She quickly gathered about herself a group of 'Spirit-filled' Christians to pray over her. These prayer warriors tolerated no negative thinking regarding my aunt's healing. They 'confessed positively' and fearlessly spoke 'the word of faith.' Being fully persuaded that 'confession brings possession,' they 'named and claimed' her complete and immediate healing. Some even said she was already healed despite the symptoms.*

---

[28] And when God does give material, temporal gifts to us, too often we value the gift above the Giver of the gift. This problem first began with Adam.

[29] The Holy Scripture is the lamp to light our feet and our pathway (Psalms 119:105).

The group received numerous prophecies and visions, which assured them that healing was inevitable.

"Shock and disbelief overtook this group of faithful intercessors when she finally died. They had genuinely and thoroughly believed they had fulfilled the conditions for healing. Because of their commitment to a 'faith formula' approach to healing, some were left with guilt feelings, suspecting that they had not believed hard enough, while others who knew better were mad at God for betraying them." [30]

It is easy for us to so desperately want something for a friend we dearly love or for a cherished family member that passion and desire clouds our thinking (Acts 21:10-11). We see this when Agabus warns the Apostle Paul against going to Jerusalem. His own protective love for Paul shaded his prophetic expression. (Luke later records what really happened in Acts chapters 26 through 28.) When we apply the spiritual gift of prophecy to personal messages for our brothers and sisters in the Lord, we must first examine our hearts, submitting ourselves to Christ and always submitting to the examination of our fellow believers. Too often, I've heard self-appointed prophets, upon hearing that a friend was starting a business, say: "Let me prophesy success for you and your business." This is a **natural** response and **we must not yield to this temptation!** Jeremiah saw this great sin in his own day and spoke against it: "Every man's own word becomes his oracle and so you distort the words of the living God, the Lord Almighty, our God" (Jeremiah 23:36).

F. Self appointed prophets

A great danger within the Christian Church in the ministries of this gift is the self-appointed prophet. They place themselves above their brothers and sisters in the Lord and offer criticism of the leadership for their failings at all levels. What they have forgotten is that without a

---

[30] Ken Blue. *Authority to Heal*, pg 43-44.

loving and generous spirit that comes with grace and gratitude, anyone can find fault with anything that goes on in the very best church. They forget that love covers a multitude of failings among brothers and sisters in Christ. They long for deeper connections and a more alive community. But they allow their longings to lead them astray. They are like parents whose children can never be good enough — the kid's grades are not as good as theirs were; the goal she scored at the soccer game was fine but what about the one she missed? Criticism disguised as a prophetic gift is in fact using the name of the Lord to advance our personal self-interests.[31] Its roots are deep in the pit of hell, eating away like a worm or moth at the very fabric of Christian community.

G. Don't mix up the gifts

Prophecy is not teaching. Typically, prophecy is not preaching. They are distinctly different, especially in that teaching and sermons are prepared in advance using various preparation methods and special tools, in addition to the inspiration and anointing of the Holy Spirit. Prophecy is an oracle, defined as very short, primarily spontaneous, and typically not prepared in advance. Is it also a prophecy when someone receives a revelation from the Lord, writes it down, and reads it to the church or includes it in a sermon? Certainly, but the gifts begin to blend in this example. Is it prophecy when the pastor receives a revelation from the Holy Spirit in the middle of his sermon and speaks it out to the congregation? Absolutely.

Typically the Sunday morning sermon from the pulpit does not include the spiritual gift of prophecy. In his book *Preaching for the Church*, Richard R. Caemmerer says that through the preacher, the Christians of his parish "all are teaching and admonishing one another." [32] Caemmerer is saying the congregants are preaching, teaching, and admonishing each other through him. In one sense he

---

[31] 1 Thessalonians 5:11 offers the means to test our hearts. Is what we are compelled to speak solidly rooted in God's love for our brothers and sisters in Christ? Will the message encourage, comfort, exhort, and build-up? See also 1 Corinthians 13:2-3.
[32] Richard R. Caemmerer. *Preaching for the Church*. Pg 56, 65.

is right because people certainly stand with their pastor, support him, pray for him, and encourage him. But we must be clear in statements like this and not leave the impression that God only speaks through the pastor who proclaims God's Word, while the people are there only to lend their ears and prayerful support.

Prophecy does not add to the Scripture. We must not ever think that prophetic messages in today's church add to Scripture as continuing revelation. Congregational prophecy will not reveal some previously unknown doctrinal truth, nor does it carry the authority of Scripture. The content of all prophetic messages must be examined to know if they are inspired by the Holy Spirit and have authority requiring obedience. The testing of prophecies is not only a Scripturally-based critique but also an opportunity for self-examination to ask, "What must we do?" If anyone attempts to elevate prophecy to the level of Scripture, they're on very thin ice. If you hear someone who claims to speak the very words of God and their message does not agree with Scripture, turn off the T.V. or change channels. Prophecy is not an expression of our personal opinion, our own understanding of Biblical truth, our interpretation, our own experience, our view of the world, a display of our personal Biblical knowledge, or a contest about who can quote the most Scripture.

H. Personal prophecies

A blatant example of the misuse of prophecy is to tell someone, using God's name as your authority, "Thus saith the Lord: You'll be married by this time next year," or "You will marry John Doe." "You're having a baby boy? Let me prophesy that he'll grow up healthy, wealthy, and wise." This is **not** typical of prophecy; it is also not a word of knowledge nor is it a word of wisdom. It is usually soulish[33] nonsense and has the potential to destroy the faith of the hearer. This kind of thing is not of the Spirit and is in fact misusing the name of God because it is highly unlikely that such a person is speaking the very words of God given by

---

[33] Soulish: This is a reference to the natural man, the soul part of man, which cannot receive spiritual gifts apart from a regenerated spirit. See glossary for further description.

revelation. As the Scripture warns us, "The prophets prophesy lies ... and my people love it this way" (Jeremiah 5:31). The prophet Micah sounds a similar warning: "If a liar and deceiver comes and says, 'I will prophesy for you plenty of wine and beer,' he would be just the prophet for this people!" (Micah 2:11). (I can hear the echo of someone's voice saying, "Now that's my kind of church.")

I. Don't avoid the hard part

We must have an abundance of spiritual discernment and strong godly leaders to keep the gift of prophecy from slipping into a soulish, people-pleasing exercise with its purpose being to advance our personal agenda or to make us feel extra spiritual. "Such 'wisdom' does not come down from heaven but is earthly, unspiritual, demonic. For where you have envy and selfish ambition, there you find disorder and every evil practice" (James 3:15-16). This kind of earthly "wisdom" only leads to shame and disgrace for God's people.

This is our challenge as Christians. We have a desire to bless and be a blessing to the Christians we rub elbows with each week. Our desire is to speak out what others want to hear. We long to offer positive affirmation and to encourage each other. We desire God's blessings for others and ourselves as well. Because of this we get a warm, fuzzy feeling in our gut and proclaim plenty of "wine and beer" for our friends so we can join the party. We prophesy a marriage so we can be invited to the wedding. We foretell blessings, hoping some will overflow upon us. But we must not do this of our own initiative, because this is using God's Holy Name in vain.

Have you noticed that many prophecies recorded in the Bible reveal sin and its consequences? The oracles of God proclaim His just and righteous judgments against sin. Prophecies often reveal sin and then God's Grace and Mercy to repentant sinners. Most important of all, the Old Testament prophets foretold the saving grace of our Lord and Savior Jesus Christ, who would give His body to be broken and His blood to be shed so that we might be forgiven and healed from the ravages of our sin.

For gatherings of believers to follow God's established order, we must be a people who are under authority, submitting ourselves to other Christians who will examine our message, testing everything by the standard of God's Word. A true and reliable test is the test of love. "If I have the gift of prophecy and can fathom all mysteries and all knowledge, and if I have a faith that can move mountains, but do not have love, I am nothing" (1 Corinthians 13:2). Holding Christ as our purpose and at the center in the ministries of spiritual gifts, beyond a doubt, will keep us from misusing this precious treasure of the kingdom of heaven.

Proof Scripture: Isaiah 56:11, Jeremiah 10:21, Ezekiel 34:8-10, Mark 1:27, 2 Peter 1:21, Revelations 22:18.

J. Misconceptions

The Church is blighted, as wheat plagued by thorns, with misinformed ideas and deceptive beliefs about the nature of the spiritual gift of prophecy. Even some great intellectual minds, blessed with vast knowledge of Biblical doctrine and theology, believe this gift was only for the apostolic age of the church. Some believe that only men who are ordained by a church organization or denomination should be the ones to exercise this gift and then primarily from a church pulpit.[34]

---

[34] Some church leaders use Article XIV or the Augsburg confession to justify limiting the exercise of the spiritual gift of prophecy, saying only ordained pastors might preach. They claim that preaching *is* prophetic ministry and allow nothing more: *"It is taught among us that nobody should publicly teach or preach or administer the sacraments in the church without a regular call."* A "Regular call" means to be called to a church and ordained as a pastor, bishop, or priest. This interpretation of the Article comes from thinking that preaching and prophesying are the same ministry, identical in nature. But they are not. No Christian church, to my knowledge, has ever forbidden preaching the Word, and it is rare to see a congregation that is contemptuous toward the ministries of preaching. Why then would Paul issue his "do not" warning (1 Thessalonians 5:20) about prophesies if there is no clear distinction between prophecy and preaching? In fact, the spiritual gift of prophecy and preaching are clearly distinct. Preaching is only a part of what is defined as an "oracle." Amos 7:16 uses two similar Hebrew words for "prophesy" and "preaching," but the definition for preaching does not include key descriptions that define prophecies as distinct. The two gifts are not the same.

Some forbid prophecies unless they are printed in the sixty-six books of the Bible, and some welcome any and all prophecies without testing the spirits or weighing the prophecy using the truths of Scripture.

The following Scripture is key to our understanding of the importance of prophecy in today's church: "Do not put out the Spirit's fire; do not treat prophecies with contempt. Test everything. Hold on to the good. Avoid every kind of evil" (1 Thessalonians 5:19-22). When we apply the context of these "final instructions" from the Apostle Paul, we can understand how the Spirit's fire is extinguished in a church. Treating prophecies with contempt! How are we contemptuous toward prophecies? When we do not teach God's people or encourage them to minister in the spiritual gift of prophecy. When we limit prophetic messages to a select few within the church, or when we refuse to allow prophetic messages to be spoken. When the church requires all prophetic messages to be preapproved. When we relegate this spiritual gift to another time, long past. We despise prophecies when we *do not* publicly test prophetic messages, throwing out the bad and holding on to the good.[35]

That verse in 1 Thessalonians also tells us that the spiritual gift of prophecy must be taught and encouraged, and that the messages must be tested so that we may hold onto the good and avoid every kind of evil. This is a clear warning that when the church abandons the spiritual gift of prophecy, they do so at the peril of putting out the Holy Spirit's fire. Please understand that our leaders are **not** putting out the Holy Spirit's fire when a prophet or prophetess comes under the loving, guiding, and evaluating authority of the pastor and elders of an established Christian church.[36] Too many of today's churches treat the ministries of the spiritual gift of prophecy with contempt. This disdain often comes to the surface when this gift is exercised by anyone other than a pastor. But a prophetic message given by means of the spiritual gift of prophecy, typically should not be blended into

---

[35] I Corinthians 14:39 is similar in its message: "Therefore, my brothers, be eager to prophesy, and do not forbid speaking in tongues."

[36] It may be good for an elder to lead in providing order, discipline, and the authoritative examination of all prophetic utterances. While this elder's function is not ordained in Scripture, it is consistent with God's call to orderly gatherings.

a sermon. When this is done it is more like inspired teaching, when in fact, it ought to be spontaneous and noteworthy.

K. Is this just a messy gift?

Allowing the ministries of the gift of prophecy in a church gathering can seem messy at times. I'm reminded of a Proverb: "An empty stable stays clean, but no income comes from an empty stable" (Proverbs 14:4 NLT). We miss God's awesome blessings for the church when we neglect this great gift for the sake of avoiding the challenges connected to it. Forbidding, ignoring, or minimizing this gift is much like keeping the barn clean by kicking out all the animals. There is no profit in that.

This gift may seem messy because of our human weakness for wanting everything neatly packaged and tied with a bow so we know what to expect each time we enter the church building. Our thinking often borders on convincing ourselves that, "If I follow this pattern for our church service, then I am satisfied that I have worshipped." In other words, "If I do this and that, I'm a godly person." But it is not within God's nature to do the same thing in the same way over and over again because He's creative in nature. I'm sure that the tribes of Israel expected God to part the waters of the Jordan River just as He parted the waters of the Red Sea, but He didn't.[37]

Orderly? Yes! Neatly fitting into our manmade box every Sunday? Not at all!

This is a good time to clear up another common misconception. A dear friend, while explaining an outburst of tongues in a public prayer time, told me, "I couldn't help it." I'm sure he was thinking that the Holy Spirit made him do it. WRONG! WRONG! NOT SO! This kind of thinking creates chaos. All of the gifts of the Spirit are subject to the one ministering by the Spirit, and we must minister in gifts of the Spirit within God's established order, in God's time.

Consider the example of traffic flow in a major city. I've driven in big cities where there is always great potential for traffic snarls.

---

[37] Compare Exodus 14:21-22 with Joshua 3:14-17.

If there were no rules of the road, no speed limits, no traffic signs, no lines to drive between, and no enforcement of the rules by police, no one would ever get anywhere. Establishing an orderly system and submitting to godly authority frees things up; until, of course, someone breaks the rules.

God has established order for the ministries of spiritual gifts (1 Corinthians 12). Each gift is subject to the one who ministers in the gift. The person who ministers in a gift is subject to the Scripture and the rules of order the church has established, and they are subject to the loving leadership and discipline of church leaders. The pastors and elders are subject to Christ and Scripture. This might seem very stifling, but in fact it allows for the excellent flowing of the gifts for strengthening the church.

One of the great errors of some churches is that they have an unreasonable fear of quenching the Holy Spirit. The result of this fear is an "everything goes" kind of thinking for fear of blocking the work of the Holy Spirit. NO! WRONG! NOT TRUE! Quite the opposite, an established order allows the "traffic" to flow in an orderly manner, and all to the glory of God.

Proof Scripture: 1 Corinthians 14:12, 33, 1 Thessalonians 5:19.

L. Caution

As a further word of caution, we must be clear in our understanding of prophecy. All prophecy must be grounded in Scripture; it must have roots deep in the Word. The hearer will do well to be a diligent student of the Word so he or she may prove what is spoken by the Word. The prophetically gifted person will do well to continually stand in the council of God, always prepared to prophesy truth (Jeremiah 23:22, Psalms 111:1). Again, no prophecy will add anything to Scripture, and it will not conflict with God's Word, but will reveal the mysteries of the cross of Jesus Christ. No true prophecy will have its root in the will or mind of man.

We must also be cautious about restricting this gift to an approved list of people who we accept as being mature students of the Word.

We must encourage those who are just starting to minister in this gift and work through the rough spots in their prophetic messages as they learn and grow. Throughout church history, some Christian leaders have tried to close doors that God has opened. We see this in communion when the people are told, "this is only for confirmed Christians."[38] Or, "You can't partake of communion with us because you speak in tongues." We see this "do it my way" attitude in baptism: "You can only be baptized after you complete this class." And regarding prophesies, "You can only prophesy if you are a called and ordained minister, and then only in the form of a sermon."

M. Biblical Order

In the exercise of the spiritual gift of prophecy, we must follow biblical limitations and instructions. We must also submit ourselves to the authority of our Lord Jesus Christ, the authority of Scripture, and the authority of godly pastors and elders within the order God has established for His church. When the gift of tongues is manifested, Scripture requires that an interpreter be present to interpret in the common language. In the same way, when a prophecy is given in public, it must be tested publicly in the spirit of Christian love. The standard for testing prophecy is the written Word of God — Holy Scripture. If any part of the prophecy does not agree with what is written from Genesis 1:1 through Revelation 22:21, that part of the message must be disregarded and the one who spoke the prophetic message must submit to the truth of the Word. "This is what he showed me: The Lord was standing by a wall that had been built true to plumb, with a plumb line in his hand" (Amos 7:7). A plumb line is similar to a level that carpenters use. A builder, even today, will use a plumb line to be sure a wall is straight up and down, or "true to plumb."

---

[38] Is it possible that we take communion in an unworthy manner (1 Corinthians 11:27) when we restrict this ordinance of worship, not encouraging all believers to partake of Christ and remember?

N. Consequences of Sin and Neglect

We must consider that the spiritual gift of prophecy may be taken from the church by our own ignorance, apostasy, refusal, or neglect. Consider Psalms 74:9: "We are given no miraculous signs; **no prophets are left**, and none of us knows how long this will be." And Lamentations 2:9b, " ...and her prophets no longer find visions from the Lord." In Amos 8:11 we hear a clear warning: "'The days are coming,' declares the Sovereign Lord, 'when I will send a famine through the land — not a famine of food or a thirst for water, but a famine of hearing the words of the Lord.'" When we treat prophecies with disdain, this gift will be taken from us.

John Calvin wrote in reference to Paul's writings in Corinthians:

> *"Today we see our own slender resources, our poverty in fact; but this is undoubtedly the punishment we deserve, as the reward for our ingratitude. For God's riches are not exhausted, nor has His liberality grown less; but we are not worthy of His largess, or capable of receiving all that He generously gives."[39]*

Calvin's expression opens my eyes to our need of repentance, and the psalmist's written words convict my heart: "Then they despised the pleasant land; they did not believe his promise. They grumbled in their tents and did not obey the Lord" (Psalm 106:24-25).

Jesus promised to send His Holy Spirit to gift and empower His people for acts of service and ministries in His church. But when we look at His precious promises, we see Goliath-sized obstacles, and we are overwhelmed with doubt. We are obstructed with supersized barriers and frozen with fear — left to grumbling under the comforters of our California king sized beds.

Jim Cymbala, in his book *Spirit Rising,* looks back on the nation of Israel and their apostasy:

---

[39] John Calvin, as quoted by Wayne Grudem. *The Gift of Prophecy in 1 Corinthians*, pg 219.

"Israel had lost the blessing and presence of their God, and amazingly, no one seemed to care. Despite God's powerful work on their behalf in the past, no one had the spiritual courage and discernment to ask, 'Where is the Lord?' Their idolatry and other sins had grieved and then forfeited God's presence, but the real tragedy was that no one missed him. Temple worship continued and animal sacrifices were offered exactly as Moses commanded, but the Spirit of God had long since gone.

"Could that be happening today? Hymns and praise choruses are sung; a sound doctrinal sermon is preached; our church services are timed and orchestrated perfectly. Too often, however, there is little of the presence and power of God that produces awe, conviction of sin, overflowing joy, and life-transforming ministry. We can easily settle for 'church' instead of God. We settle for a paradigm and deny the power. And every succeeding generation shaped in that mold makes it harder for anyone to dare ask, 'Where is the Lord?'"[40]

In the strength of the Spirit of Jesus, we must press on to fulfill Christ's purpose and plan for the good of the church and His kingdom. Proverbs 29:18 says, "Where there is no revelation, the people cast off restraint." The KJV says, "the people perish." This Scripture may well be paraphrased, "Where there is no revelation of Jesus Christ, the people cast away the restraining fear of God." The people dry up spiritually without a strong prophetic ministry, and wherever the spiritual gift of prophecy is ignored, despised, minimized or rejected, you will find a valley of dry bones.

Proof Scripture: Ezekiel 7:26, Ezekiel 16:9-15, Micah 3:7, 2 Timothy 1:6, 1 Corinthians chapters 12, 13 & 14, 2 Corinthians 11:4.

We are called to turn away from human inclinations and self-inspired, self-directed service and ministry. The Scriptures instruct us to put aside human reasoning that leads us to please others rather

---

[40] Jim Cymbala. *Spirit Rising*, pg 191-192.

than ministering in the power of the Spirit. Church leaders are called to teach, train, and encourage those whom the Spirit chooses to gift with spiritual gift of prophecy. As Christians, we are encouraged to clarify our understanding of the spiritual gift of prophecy so that we may minister powerfully and effectively in the spirit, by means of the Spirit, and to affect people for good and for all eternity. In Christ we have victorious faith to overcome these human failings — and by means of this sin-conquering faith, Christ will be exalted in the ministries of the spiritual gift of prophecy.

Your Journey Journal

Chapter 3: Christ the Center

A.   What makes Christians fallible in the ministries of the spiritual gift of prophecy?

B.   What are the dangers of "people pleasing" prophecies?

C.   What are the consequences of rejecting or neglecting this precious spiritual gift given to the church?

Your Journal Notes:

PART 2

Prophecy at Work in the Church

"These gates lead to the presence of the LORD, and the godly enter there" (Psalms 118:20 NLT). Step through this gate with me to encounter the Holy Spirit manifesting the living, active presence of Jesus Christ in a gathering of believers. As we step through the gateway, we hear Jesus give a clear and timeless call that reveals the way He shows His presence in the world and in the church today. "As long as it is day, **we** must do the works of him who sent me. Night is coming, when no one can work. While I am in the world, I am the light of the world" (John 9:4-5, emphasis added). Jesus does not manifest Himself in His earthly body today. But it is still His desire to manifest His presence. When Jesus said "WE," this has to be the biggest "WE" of all time. "WE" includes all the redeemed, all who are called by His name, and all who are His disciples. This includes Christians from the church's beginning all the way up to our day. Jesus told His followers: "You are the light of the world" (Matthew 5:14). In baptism, we are made "one" with Christ, a part of His body, and today "WE" are the working parts of His manifest presence in the world. The spiritual gift of prophecy is a major part of His presence, made real to those who will hear and believe.

After Philip met Jesus, he found Nathaniel and said, "Come and see." In this chapter you will see how your Lord has called you to be His ambassadors, including men, women, sons, and daughters (Joel 2:28). You'll clearly see that prophecy can have only one source, and then we'll answer the question: What are the qualifications for those who will prophesy in a gathering of believers?

1

Christ's Empowering Work

Many ancient kingdoms sent out envoys to represent their interests to the nations around them. Modern countries send diplomats to establish embassies in every capitol of the world. The Kingdom of Heaven began this practice, as God called people He chose to be messengers of His kingdom to every tribe, nation, people, and tongue. There is great honor in speaking on behalf of God's Kingdom, and yet, in our limited way of thinking, we attempt to exclude some people whom the Spirit calls to serve in the gifts they are given. We must not be like the Jewish Sanhedrin and attempt to stop what God has ordained. Peter and John declared this truth with great boldness: "As for us, we cannot help speaking about what we have seen and heard" (Acts 4:19). A prophetic message given by the Spirit is like fire in the belly of those who God calls, and the message will not be repressed.

A. Ambassadors

Those who ministered as ancient Israel's Prophets served as God's ambassadors to people, tribes, cities, and nations. In the Old Testament we find different levels of prophets. Some examples include Moses, the Prophet, and then Aaron who was Moses' prophet (Exodus 7:1), appointed to deliver to the people the messages that Moses received from God. Elijah had a company or school of prophets that may well have been "deputized" to proclaim God's messages that came through Elijah. Sacred musicians are said to have prophesied (1 Chronicles 25:1). In the New Testament, the "prophets" are men and women, sons and daughters, who are empowered and gifted by the Holy Spirit to proclaim in word or song the oracles of God, as ambassadors for the church.

Those who minister in the spiritual gift of prophecy typically speak from immediate inspiration, and always by the power of the Spirit, illuminating the words of God to the church. Acts 13:1 says that Barnabas, Simeon, Lucius, and Manaen were teachers or prophets in the church at Antioch. God has given to His church first apostles, and then prophets. We must make a distinction between the office of prophet and those who are given the spiritual gift of prophecy, because the office of prophet has a greater responsibility. But **no** prophets in the New Testament Church are on the same level as Isaiah, Jeremiah, Ezekiel, David, Joel, Amos, and the others who recorded God's actual words in Scripture. Today's prophets and prophetesses must not claim that their words have the authority of Scripture;[41] but they commonly have Christ's authority for the content of their message. This distinction is important to grasp because we must be clear that as we minister in the spiritual gift of prophecy we do not add to, subtract from, or in any way change what is written from Genesis through Revelation.

Proof Scripture: 1 Corinthians 12:28, Ephesians 2:20, Revelations 18:20, Acts 21:9, 2 Kings 2:7, 15.

B. Prophetesses

Old Testament prophecies make it clear that women will prophesy in the last days, in the age of the church. "And afterward, I will pour out my Spirit on all people. Your sons and daughters will prophesy, your old men will dream dreams, your young men will see visions. Even on my servants, both men and women, I will pour out my Spirit in those days" (Joel 2:28-29).[42] There are several prophetesses mentioned

---

[41] When claiming their words are the word of God, prophets will be speaking straight out of the Scriptures, quoting passages, and possibly amplifying God's Word to His people.

[42] Compare this to Acts 2:17-19.

in Scripture and one example of a woman who held the office of Prophet. Examples are Miriam, Deborah[43] and Huldah; and in the New Testament, Anna, Elisabeth, and Mary, and then the four daughters of Philip who seem to have ministered in a time of prophetic revelation. The Apostle Paul's writing regarding prophecy in the congregation does not restrict prophesying to men.[44] Prophecies offered by men, women, sons, or daughters, as with any message given by the Holy Spirit through the spiritual gift of prophecy, must be examined or evaluated by the congregation. Again, this is not only a critique of the prophetic message, but an examination of the hearer in light of the prophetic message, an opportunity to ask, "What must we do?"

It's worth repeating: all who serve in this gift, whether men or women, must prophesy "under authority." They are under the loving, caring authority of pastors and elders who are under the shepherd-like authority of Christ, the Head of the Church. When prophesying, men must to submit to Christ, pastors, and elders. And women do well to position themselves under the protective covering and the authority of Christ, their husbands, fathers, or elders.[45] A protective covering of a husband, pastor, or elder is important for women who prophesy. Especially if a woman prophesies exposing a sin in the congregation, she will need a protective covering, just as a man will need the protective covering of the pastor and elders.

---

[43] Judges 4:4, "Deborah, a prophetess, the wife of Lappidoth, was leading Israel at the time." This was an exceptional time in Israel, and God found an exceptional woman to lead His people. It is also worth noting that Junia is mentioned by the Apostle Paul as "outstanding among the apostles" in Romans 16:7. Typically, apostles would serve in the spiritual gift of prophecy.

[44] 1 Corinthians 11:1-16 offers a clear understanding of God's order of authority in the church. Some read this and claim that Paul is writing about traditions of the early church, and modern traditions are not the same. My encouragement to you is to read this Scripture and phrase by phrase ask the question; "Has this changed or not?" In verse 6, "[I]f it is a disgrace for a woman to have her hair cut off" — this has changed. For those things that have not changed, Paul is offering instructions that are applicable even today. 1st Corinthians chapter eleven must also be read with a clear historical context. This context may be found in the book, *Let My People Go: A Call to End the Oppression of Women in the Church*, by Bob Edwards.

[45] This doesn't mean you cannot minister in the gift of prophecy in a gathering where a pastor or elder isn't present. You can honor and respect the leadership of the church while prophesying anywhere the Spirit leads you to do so.

Based on the principle of God's established order, Paul offers his instructions: "For this reason a woman ought to have a symbol of authority on her head" (1 Corinthians 11:10). [46] Is this "symbol" only for the early church, in their time, in their culture? This whole concept of women prophesying was very radical because it was contrary to Hebrew traditions. In Jesus' time, women were forbidden even to touch the Torah scrolls or to take part in discussions that followed Scripture readings in the synagogue. [47] Examine 1 Corinthians 11:1-16 to discern what was custom in their day and what is unchangeable and timeless.

Proof Scripture: Ephesians 5:21, Colossians 3:18-24, Acts 21:8-9, 1 Corinthians 11:3-16.

C. The Source

Those who minister in the spiritual gift of prophecy receive their messages from God at times spontaneously, sometimes in visions and dreams. But God spoke directly to His prophet Moses (Numbers 12:8). We can see this clearly when we compare Numbers 24:2-16, Joel 2:28, Acts 10:11-13, Revelations 1:10-20. These revelations were occasionally accompanied with overpowering manifestations of the Spirit; and at other times they were simply breathed into the prophet's spirit [48] by

---

[46] God's order for family and church has not changed since the Apostle Paul wrote: "There is neither Jew nor Gentile, neither slave nor free, nor is there male and female, for you are all one in Christ Jesus" (Galatians 3:28). This principle of equality applies to a woman praying and prophesying in the church and is still excellent in every way. We must all be in submission to the equality God has established. Paul does not tell us what that sign of authority must be, because this sign may change from culture to culture. It is for us to decide. This symbol openly declares that the woman who is praying or prophesying is under the protective covering of Christ, her husband, father, pastor, or an elder.

[47] Ann Spangler & Jean E. Syswerda. *Women of the Bible*, pg 423.

[48] We do not practice or teach that a prophet's mind must be a blank slate or clear of any thoughts for the Spirit of the Lord to give His prophetic word. This kind of thinking is attributable to Eastern religions that teach people to meditate, clearing their minds of all things. On the contrary, prophecies are most often inspired with the hearing of Scripture when preachers proclaim Jesus Christ or when one is thinking and meditating on Scripture.

the Spirit of God. The prophets were compelled by the Spirit to deliver their messages to the kings, princes, and priests whom the messages concerned, or to people at large, in writing, or by word of mouth and in public places, often with proving miracles or with symbolic actions designed to explain and enforce their messages (Isaiah 20:1-6, Jeremiah 7:2-3, 19:1-15, Ezekiel 3:10-11).

There is an Old Testament example of the outpouring of a prophetic utterance when the Holy Spirit came upon Saul as he was chosen to be king: "The Spirit of the Lord will come upon you in power, and you will prophesy with them; and you will be changed into a different person" (1 Samuel 10:6).

We find in 2 Samuel 7:1-17 a perfect and clear Old Testament example of the use of prophecy that is still applicable in the New Testament church. God had given King David rest from all his enemies, so David said to Nathan the prophet, "Here I am, living in a house of cedar, while the ark of God remains in a tent." Nathan sees that David wishes to honor God and replies, "Whatever you have in mind, go ahead and do it, for the Lord is with you." But that night Nathan was redirected by the Lord saying, not David, but his son will "build a house for my Name."

David wished to honor God. Nathan knew that God was with David and he thought it was a good thing; but God revealed His purpose, plan, and desire to the prophet Nathan at night, and in the morning he reported all the words of the revelation to King David.

Our prayer: *Lord, help us; we need Your revelation power at work among your people so we may walk according to Your will, purpose, plan, and desire.*

D. Qualifications:

By the grace of our Lord Jesus Christ, should His Holy Spirit determine or will this gift for you, you are qualified. This doesn't mean that you can become a self-proclaimed prophet. If you believe the Spirit has given or will give this gift to you, the most trustworthy confirmation and empowerment of this gift will be through the ministry of a pastor,

Presbyter (1 Timothy 4:14),[49] or an elder with the gift of presbytery, and most likely by the ministry of laying on of hands. Remember this foundational principle: everything is established by two or three witnesses (2 Corinthians 13:1). At the same time it's important to remember that God will impart any spiritual gift He so chooses to whomever He chooses, at any time He chooses, and especially to those who ask. The above reference to presbyters is offered as the most desirable way to receive a spiritual gift.

Many believe the minimum requirements of a Christian ministering in the gift of prophecy can be summarized as follows:

(1) The prophetic message must be spoken clearly and not in vague or general terms that can be subject to various interpretations. Example: "This year God will do a great thing in your life," is not a prophecy or even a word of knowledge. Someone may speak in this way, trying to be vague because they don't understand what God has revealed to them. It would be better if they waited for God to open their understanding before speaking out.

To encourage those who are new in the use of this gift, we must offer opportunities to say what is revealed to them, as they understand it, knowing that they will become more proficient in this gift, and with encouragement and practice the anointing will increase. No one will throw rocks at those who make a mistake.

(2) It's important for those ministering in the prophetic gift to do their best, not allowing the words they speak to be influenced, colored, or shaded by their own beliefs, experience, opinions, dogmas, or theology. This is an easy, very human mistake because the one prophesying chooses the words, phrases, and expressions with which they communicate the message they have heard or seen. The point is this: do your best and remember that God is gracious and merciful to fallible beings with contrite hearts.

(3) Prophetic messages must never contradict Scripture.

Proof Scripture: 1 Corinthians 14:32.

---

[49] The Greek word for elders is: πρεσβυτέριον *presbyterion.*

Walk with me through this gate called "Prophecy" and enter a garden where we hear the sweet song of Jesus. We hear His precious words — a new refrain to our ears — and we blend our voices to speak what He is speaking, and to sing what He is singing. Our voices ring with His words. Words to call us back from our wandering ways. Words of life, peace, comfort, strength, and healing. As we sing in harmony with our Lord Jesus, His living, active presence is revealed to all who will hear His words spoken in the congregation. In the ministries of this spiritual gift, we become like a precious jewel reflecting light in the darkness; the night flees as the Light of Life shines out. The turmoil of our lives is stilled, like roiling waves turned to a sea still as glass. (See Matthew 8:23-37, Revelation 15:2.)

All whom the Spirit calls, men, women, sons, and daughters, come join in, speaking His words and singing a new song with our Lord Jesus, so that Jesus Christ, our Lord and Savior, is revealed in the congregation.

Your Journey Journal

Q & A Chapter 1
Christ's Empowering Work

A.   Who can prophesy in gatherings of Christian believers?

B.   How does a word of prophecy come to the person who prophesies?

C.   What are the qualifications for ministries in the spiritual gift of prophecy?

Your Journal Notes:

2

Christ's Living, Active Presence

Opposition confronted the prophet Nehemiah on every side.[50] He was the king's cupbearer in the Persian court, and by the hand of God, the king approved his journey to Jerusalem to rebuild the walls. Yet obstacles stood in his way no matter where he turned. Sanbalat, Tobiah, and their co-conspirators fought against him. Nehemiah's own people were unruly and easily discouraged because they had to work with one hand and grip their swords in the other. Surely he was tempted to give up. It would have been easy to say, "Listen up people. Put your shovels and swords away. This isn't God's time for rebuilding the temple."

God has not changed. We too must stand and armor up to do all that God has called us to do in the power of His might, by His command, and in the strength of the Spirit. We must face what comes against us and fearlessly serve and minister according to the good gifts the Holy Spirit empowers in us.

A. Is prophecy for today?

Jesus' teachings make reference to prophets in the age of the church soon to come. We also find many references to prophets who serve in the church after the death and resurrection of Christ. Christians believe that the Holy Spirit leads people to faith in Jesus, gives them the ability to walk in the Spirit, and gives spiritual gifts to Christians

---

[50] This historic event is recorded in the book of Nehemiah.

for the good of the church as a witness of God's saving grace at work among His people. These clearly include the charismatic or utterance gifts such as prophecy.

Christians holding to an opinion called cessationism[51] believe these gifts were given only in the early church and ceased after the last apostle died. They believe that God only speaks to His people today through the written Word, the Holy Bible. I once heard a prominent radio preacher ask his audience, "Have any of you ever heard God speak?" The congregation's answer was to laugh, as if it was laughable to think it possible. But consider this. "[F]or he who makes it trusts in his own creation; he makes idols that cannot speak" (Habakkuk 2:18). May I suggest that if you do not hear God speak to you, it's possible that you have a god of your own making? Without a doubt, to all in whom His Spirit dwells, God speaks by means of His Holy Spirit. This precious communion is infinitely intimate and beautiful as His voice resonates within our spirit.

How does God speak to His people today? First and foremost through the written words of Scripture. God's Word speaks to us and the Holy Spirit opens our understanding of the Word. The Spirit inspires the Word planted in our hearts and whispers truth into our spirit. Not everyone is able to hear God's whispers in every moment of their lives. In these instants, God will inspire His Word in the present moment, spontaneously inspiring those who minister in the spiritual gift of prophecy to speak His words to a gathering of believers.[52]

Elihu, speaking to Job, reveals that it is God's nature to speak to those He created: "For God speaks in one way, and in two, though people do not perceive it" (Job 33:14). Be assured that God has not changed. The nation of Israel took great pride in having all of God's law written on the scrolls, and yet they killed, stoned, and silenced God's prophets. Today we proudly claim to have the complete canon of

---

[51] The theology of cessationism is dangerously close to Deism. To say that God gave us His inspired Word in the Holy Scripture and then ceased to speak to His people in the moment, every day of their lives is clearly a serious error.

[52] Remember, it is not the Spirit's nature to single out one person by name for correction in a public gathering. Prophetic messages are for all to hear and thereby examine themselves. God will, on occasion, point out people by name when He is calling them to a mission, ministry, or service.

Scripture, and demand that those who would minister in the spiritual gift of prophecy be silent. This is to our shame and we are called to repentance.

The world turns and the seasons change. The climate changes. The boundary lines of the nations change; but we have a solid Rock to stand on. We serve God who does not change (Malachi 3:6). Scripture gives no credence to the teaching that charismatic gifts are no longer available to the church (Romans 12:6-8). Recorded history of the orthodox Christian Church contradicts the belief that gifts have ceased. It is unimaginable that God would give good gifts to His church for the purpose of building up His people and then later say, "Oh, sorry. You can't have that anymore." The book of Joel makes clear that the gift of prophecy "in those days" was for all of "those days" and not for just the beginning of "those days."

Proof Scripture: Matthew 10:40-41 & 23:34, John 13:20 & 15:20, Acts 11:25-30, 13:1 & 15:32.

B. Be fearless

> *"And you, son of man, do not be afraid of them or their words. Do not be afraid, though briers and thorns are all around you and you live among scorpions. Do not be afraid of what they say or terrified by them, though they are a rebellious house. You must speak my words to them, whether they listen or fail to listen, for they are rebellious." (Ezekiel 2:6)*

Note the differences between Old Testament prophecy and congregational prophecy. Ezekiel was told, "You must speak my words." In congregational prophecy the Holy Spirit does not typically give us the exact words to say, but we choose the words to speak, interpreting and proclaiming what God has revealed to us. God will not violate the personalities he gave us. Yet in this process of word choice, we must not spin the message to please the hearer. If we try to please the hearer for fear of the crowd rather than fearing God, we're digging ourselves into a deep trap. Jesus encourages us: "Do not be afraid of those who kill the body but cannot kill the soul. Rather be afraid of the one who can destroy both soul and body in hell" (Matthew 10:28).

Proof Scripture: Deuteronomy 1:17, Proverbs 29:25, Jeremiah 1:8, Isaiah 51:12.

C. Exercising the gift

What happens in the church if a pastor allows Christians the opportunity to minister in the gifts of the Spirit in church gatherings? Some of the challenges we often face in the exercise of the utterance gifts may be somewhat similar to businesses owners who do not diligently manage every aspect of their business. The result is ruin — bankruptcy for the business. In the Church, all spiritual gifts require wise, diligent, and godly shepherds to offer leadership and discipline as the gifts are ministered, not controlling but allowing for the spiritual gifts to function in an orderly manner for the good of the whole Church. Without loving shepherding, accountability, and discipline, the spiritual gifts run amok and become messy, even disturbing. [53] In a church where men and women minister in the gift of prophecy, there must also be someone who has the gift of spiritual discernment to be sure that the source of the prophetic utterance is the Holy Spirit and not another spirit or rooted in selfish ambition.

But how does it look when this spiritual gift is manifested in a gathering of Christian believers? Attempting to list every possible manifestation that the Holy Spirit will inspire is an impossible task. But it will be helpful to see a few examples.

All Christians who listen to the Spirit of Jesus minister in a common form of prophetic ministry. Moses said, "I wish that all the Lord's people were prophets" (Numbers 11:29). This common ministry doesn't mean you are gifted in the Spirit with the spiritual gift of prophecy.

---

[53] We don't stop driving our car because someone else had a bad accident. Never should we disregard the imperatives of Scripture because they haven't worked for someone else. We must learn from others' mistakes and push forward.

Common prophetic-style ministries may come at a time when you are praying for a friend. While praying, the Spirit whispers into your spirit a Scripture and leads you to call your friend or give the verse to him or her in a special greeting card. A stronger example of a common prophetic style of ministry may be during a Bible study when the Holy Spirit reveals a truth to you while the Holy Scripture is being read, and He urges you to share that insight. Or while you're praying with others a sense of urgency comes over you to pray for a missionary friend in Mongolia. This kind of ministry ought to be common in the church today.

Ministering in the fullness of the spiritual gift of prophecy may look like this: You're attending a home Bible study and the Spirit compels you to proclaim something revealed to you, and what you express comes out as a two or three minute oracle, encouraging, admonishing, and strengthening your brothers and sisters in the Lord. Or the Holy Spirit will bring something to mind during a worship service and you know you must share this truth. Perhaps while Scripture is being read a revelation of truth washes over you like a wave and the Spirit is urging you to express this truth to the gathering. Another manifestation of the gift of prophecy would be when someone sees clearly, by the Spirit, that a brother or sister should step out in a service or ministries of the church and then speaking out (at an appropriate time), encouraging them to do so.

How do you know when the Holy Spirit is giving you a prophetic message? You must first know that you have been gifted in this ministry, and the best way to know is through the ministry of a Presbyter. This assurance bolsters you with confidence to minister in this awesome gift.

It would be impossible to list every way you may know the Spirit's leading. First you should ask yourself, "Am I standing in the council of God?" You may know the Spirit's leading when there is a burning, glowing warmth welling up inside you. "Is not my word like a fire?" (Jeremiah 23:29). "But when I was silent and still, not even saying anything good, my anguish increased. My heart grew hot within me, and as I meditated, the fire burned; then I spoke with my tongue" (Psalm 39:3). "His word is in my heart like a fire" (Jeremiah 20:9). Most clear of all these Scriptures: "The lion has roared — who will not fear? The Sovereign Lord has spoken — who can but prophesy?" (Amos 3:8). You may at times get a sense as if warm oil is flowing from within you. It's likely that when the Spirit reveals something to you, a feeling of urgency wells up in you until you speak it out, a sense of great joy at the thought of sharing, and the list could go on and on. We are each unique before the Lord and He will lead us in a way that is unique to us.

The final point is clear and simple. You must not limit God by claiming He doesn't speak, manifesting His living, active presence among His people, only because you have not heard Him speak. To deny that God speaks is to deny the truth of God's Word, and then you must also deny the precious spiritual gifts held out to you in Jesus' nail scarred hands. Your faith will become stronger as you exercise the faith given to you. To be strengthened in your spiritual gift, it is necessary to fearlessly exercise the gift. When God's message burns within you, speak it out at an appropriate time and place and the fire will burn even brighter.

Your Journey Journal

Q & A Chapter 2
Christ's Living, Active Presence

A.   Why is prophecy relevant in gatherings of believers in today's church?

B.   What are the dangers of being fearful when ministering in this spiritual gift?

C.   What challenges must be faced for this gift to be the most effective in the church?

Your Journal Notes:

3

Christ's Word Present in Prophecy

Jesus gathered disciples around Him who were theologically illiterate; they lacked credentials and had no accolades behind their names to recommend them. Yet after three years of Jesus University they were trained, prepared to do the work of the Kingdom of Heaven. When they received the gifting and empowering of the Holy Spirit, they spoke with great power and authority. They were passionate in testifying of the resurrected Jesus Christ, who was present with them. They paid a great price for their boldness. Chains, prison bars, lashings, and beatings besieged them at every turn.

But Jesus' disciples, seeing through the eyes of faith, pressed on because they could see the great benefits of ministering the resurrected Christ to those who were wandering in spiritual darkness. As they poured themselves out in the service and ministries of the Spirit, they continually came before the Spirit of Grace to be refilled again so they could be strong and powerful in the work they were called to do.

A. Encouragement to ask for this gift

We are weak vessels and ineffective instruments. But God chooses to shape us and refine us into useful vessels from which we are to be a demonstration of His power and might — as witnesses of the power of His Holy Name. The spiritual gift of prophecy is an authoritative and useful means that God has chosen to minister to His church to comfort, encourage, console, build up, teach, edify, admonish, correct, and reveal the mysteries of His Son, our Lord Jesus Christ. If you don't know someone gifted in the ministry of a Presbyter, that's okay — go ahead and ask for the desire God has put in your heart. The Apostle Paul's words urge us today more than ever: "Now eagerly desire the greater gifts" (1 Corinthians 12:31).

How can we reject or bury so great a gift given to us at such great cost?

B. Hazardous duty

If it is your desire to minister in the spiritual gift of prophecy, you ought to first count the cost (Luke 14:28). The prophet Jeremiah was threatened with death, he was thrown into a muddy cistern, and he was imprisoned (Jeremiah 26, 38, and 39), because the king and the people did not want to hear what God was saying through him. In the same way, when you minister in the prophetic gift, you are carrying the heavy weapons of the kingdom of God. In Matthew, Jesus speaks of the end result of many an Old Testament prophet's labors. He talks about all the prophets the Israelites killed, "from the blood of righteous Abel to the blood of Zechariah son of Berekiah, whom you murdered between the temple and the altar" (Matthew 23:35). Jesus warned of the hazards: "Therefore I am sending you prophets and wise men and teachers. Some of them you will kill and crucify; others you will flog in your synagogues and pursue from town to town" (Matthew 23:34). Jesus grieved: "O Jerusalem, Jerusalem, you who kill the prophets and stone those sent to you, how often I have longed to gather your children together, as a hen gathers her chicks under her wings, but you were not willing" (Matthew 23:37).[54]

When you speak to people, proclaiming to them what the Spirit has revealed to you, you will not be their favorite. "They say to the seers, 'See no more visions!' and to the prophets, 'Give us no more

---

[54] I am not suggesting that present day prophets might be physically stoned to death. There are many ways to throw "rocks" that are intended to hurt almost as much.

visions of what is right! Tell us pleasant things, prophesy illusions.[55] Leave this way, get off this path, and stop confronting us with the Holy One of Israel!'" (Isaiah 30:10).

When you are an instrument of the Spirit of Jesus, called upon to proclaim His revealed message to His people, you must be armored up, i.e. you must put on all of the armor of God (Ephesians 6:10-18). This is not your armor with all the rust, chinks and dents in it. This is God's armor, and it fits and protects each one of us perfectly.

While it is unlikely that a church will throw you into a well behind the church, stone you or kill you, you may no longer be welcomed. You may be questioned, you may be marginalized, you may be preached at, you may be pushed aside, you may have Scripture aimed at you like stones, you may be the object of gossip, and you may be falsely accused. Have you ever been frozen out of a group of friends or become so isolated that you're left out of everything? No one talks to you? Consider the cost before you open your mouth. Consider, are friendships and fellowship what you value most of all, or will you speak the truth in love no matter the consequences? Will you proclaim what God compels you to speak by the prompting of the Spirit?[56]

Paul makes clear our connection with Christ's afflictions: "Now I rejoice in what was suffered for you, and I fill up in my flesh what is still lacking in regard to Christ's afflictions for the sake of his body, which is the church" (Colossians 1:24). Our afflictions do not in any way add to the perfectly sufficient and atoning work of our Lord Jesus Christ for our redemption. But Jesus also suffered that the church may be brought into being as His body. We too, like Christ, may be afflicted in the building of Christ's church and the Kingdom of Heaven.

We know that a mother gives birth in great pain. Bonnie has a daughter, Trisha, and she is the spitting image of her mother. She has her mom's blue eyes, her mom's curly blond hair; she talks like her

---

[55] Some people may only want you to prophesy prosperity, health and healing, smooth sailing, and good times ahead, but this is right only when this is what God is saying to His people in the moment.

[56] Ministries in spiritual gifts are best when ministered under loving, caring, and godly leadership — the covering of the church. This is ideal. When the leadership of a church does not provide this shield, God may call you to minister and serve in another place.

mom, walks like her mom, and thinks like her mom. Bonnie has long forgotten the pain of childbirth, but Trisha must suffer growing pains, the pains of falling down and skinning her knee when learning to walk, and the pain of crashing when the training wheels come off the bicycle. And then there is the pain of rejection when her friends refuse to play with her. Bonnie shares in this pain in a very real way, but Trisha is the one who must bear up under this suffering, even under mom's watchful eye. We can liken this to Christ's sufferings that gave birth to the church and our sufferings for the growing church and expanding Kingdom of God. While this is true for all Christians, it is most certainly true for those who minister in the spiritual gift of prophecy.

C. The benefits

The church is blessed with more benefits from this spiritual gift of prophecy than we can possibly imagine. Knowing that this discussion of those benefits will be incomplete at best, let's begin.

Active participation in the spiritual gift of prophecy among the priesthood of believers (1 Peter 2:9) indicates a healthy local church. All spiritual gifts given to the church by the Holy Spirit, when they are ministered among the people, are witnesses, powerful proof that God's saving grace is at work among His people. We are called to be His witnesses, offering proof of the power of His Holy Name (John 15:26-27, 1 Corinthians 1:4-7).

These Scriptures must be considered in a church where God is not speaking through prophetic gifts:

> *"Is it not because I have long been silent that you do not fear me?" (Isaiah 57: 11b)*

> *"In those days the word of the Lord was rare; there were not many visions." (1 Samuel 3:1)*

When God speaks to His church through those ministering in this gift, a breath of reverence, awe, and reverent fear of the Lord comes to rest among His people. Common prophetic ministry is refreshing in a church, but the ministry of the spiritual gift of prophecy builds, strengthens, and admonishes the church, laying bare secrets of the heart. This is a powerful ministry revealing the living, active presence of our Lord Jesus. Prophetic ministries cause people to "fall down and worship God, exclaiming, 'God is really among you!'" (1 Corinthians 14:25).

Through the ministry of prophecy, Scripture comes alive, exposing sin, convincing us of sin, convicting us of sin (1 Corinthians 14:25), opening our eyes to our depravity, opening our ears to hear, and opening our understanding to know the resurrected Christ.[57] Through the ministry of the spiritual gift of prophecy we come into an awareness of the Lord's active, immediate presence among us (Joshua 3:9-10).

It is too easy for us to slide into unconsciously thinking that He wrote a letter to us (the Bible) more than two thousand years ago to reveal Himself, forgetting He is alive, ever present and dwelling in us, His temple — RIGHT NOW! God is not the One who spoke to us only in the past; He is speaking to His people today, in this very moment. It is God's present voice that makes Scripture speak with power and effect in the hearts of believers. Because of our dullness, because we perceive God as silent, because we think God is distant, we do not fear the Lord in our moments of temptation and sin. This spiritual gift to the church changes all that.

Through the ministries of congregational prophecy, God has provided another means to edify and strengthen His church. When this spiritual gift is common practice among believers in a local church, they will stop being religious consumers and join the work of building up the church. This gift, as all the gifts of the Spirit ministered in a church body do, builds and strengthens the fabric of Christian community. Still another great benefit of allowing the spiritual gift of prophecy in a worship gathering is that worship moves beyond a

---

[57] Prophetic ministries must not displace ministering the Word and sacraments, prayer, the singing of Psalms, hymns, and spiritual songs. Prophetic utterances offered from within the congregation must instead strengthen these long standing church ministries.

spectator event with congregants singing only prescribed songs and mouthing prearranged words. The operation of this gift brings life and vitality to worship and provides a powerful demonstration of God's active presence at work among His people.

Prophecies serve to expose sin and bring a heart to repentance. "But if an unbeliever or an inquirer comes in while everyone is prophesying, they are convicted of sin and are brought under judgment by all, as the secrets of their hearts are laid bare" (1 Corinthians 14:24-25). In this Scripture we see prophetic ministries serving to reveal the secrets of the heart of an unbeliever, convincing them of sin and calling to repentance.

This is another reason prophecy must not be limited. How many pastors or evangelists could have been stopped in their sin if the spiritual gift of prophecy had been at work in their congregations? Think of all the Christian leaders whose hearts could have been brought to repentance if this gift had been functioning in their churches. Instead their sins were exposed before the whole world and the church was brought into disgrace. "The visions of your prophets were false and worthless; they did not expose your sin to ward off your captivity" (Lamentations 2:14). We see an even greater benefit when this spiritual gift is operating in a local church. The people, elders, deacons, and pastors are warned of doctrinal error and brought to repentance.

We see a clear example of a prophet working in the capacity of exposing sin in 2 Samuel 12:1-13. Nathan confronts David face to face and brings David to see his sin and say, "I have sinned against the Lord."

Is it possible that our All Wise God and Father established the spiritual gift of prophecy as a check and balance system within the church? Could the church have avoided many of the scandals that have brought dishonor to the Name of Christ? Because we are all fallible human beings whom positions of power and money tend to corrupt, we need the Holy Spirit to speak through various members of the body rather than one man. This accountability is sorely needed in the church, and wise pastors and elders will encourage this gift. Sins are easily hidden from our brothers and sisters that we only see on Sunday mornings after we've showered, shaved, and changed into our Sunday morning attitude. But not so when the spiritual gift of prophecy is at work among us and the "secrets of our hearts are laid bare."

How many times have you been searching, earnestly praying to know the heart and mind of God in a matter? You find encouragement in the study of Scripture, you feel encouraged when you pray, but you just don't know for sure what God desires of you regarding this issue. An excellent guiding principle is found here. "[E]very matter may be established by the testimony of two or three witnesses" (Matthew 18:16; see also, Deuteronomy 19:15, 2 Corinthians 13:1). Scripture will witness to you, a friend may be encouraging you, but wouldn't it be so good to hear a sure third witness giving an unbiased word of encouragement? The spiritual gift of prophecy at work among the congregation will also serve in this capacity. Please remember that we are not to use a prophecy as our sole guide. It is not our crystal ball. It is not the "light" for our pathway, but it can be an excellent additional witness.

D. Receiving the spiritual gift of prophecy

This spiritual gift is to be desired above many others, and is a gift of grace[58] that cannot be earned. The gifts are not like a "Merit Badge," or a "Medal of Honor." There is no method, no ceremony, no ritual, no formula, no special prayer to pray, no to do list. But we are to present ourselves as a "living sacrifice:" "Present your bodies as a living sacrifice, holy and acceptable to God, which is your spiritual worship"

---

[58] (Greek for Charism is χαρίσμα.) In the theology of Christendom a **charism** in general is any gift that flows from God to man. The word also means any of the spiritual gifts granted to a Christian to perform his or her ministry or service in a gathering of believers. In the narrowest sense, it is a theological term for the extraordinary graces, gifts of the Spirit given to individual Christians for serving others.

(Romans 12:1 NRSV).[59], [60] Allow our Lord Jesus Christ to prepare you as a bride prepares for her Bridegroom.

The gift of prophecy is given as the Spirit determines. But we should not be passive about receiving it. Instead we ought to desire it and earnestly ask "the Gift" who graces us with spiritual gifts. The Apostle Paul encourages us to be eager for the gift of prophecy. The Old Testament prophets spoke of this day: "They will come trembling in awe to the Lord, and they will receive his good gifts in the last days" (Hosea 3:5b). This Scripture does not say that *if* they come in the "fear of the Lord," **then** they will receive His good gifts. Instead this verse shows us that the people's hearts were right as they came before the Lord and He graciously gave them good gifts. Our Lord Jesus took care of all the "ifs" and "thens" on our behalf.

Remember, God desires to give His bride precious adornments, beautifying adornments, and kingdom jewels of inestimable value because of the power of His overwhelming love for us.

---

[59] It is commonly taught in a few denominations that a Christian ought to prepare him or herself to receive spiritual gifts. The steps are; a. Confess all known sin. b. Repent of any remaining sin in their lives. c. Trust Christ to forgive those sins. d. Commit every area of your life to the Lord's service. e. Completely yield him or herself fully to God. f. Believe that Christ is going to empower them in a new way and equip them with new gifts for ministry. (Source: *Systematic Theology* Dr. Wayne Grudem, pg 779.) All of these things are excellent, and in fact, a — e are at the very core of the Spirit's work of salvation in our heart of hearts, as repentance joins hands with faith for our salvation. Be encouraged to complete these steps at any time — not as a formula, but to examine your Christian walk. Just remember that these were part of justification and included in sanctification and not a formula for receiving the gifts of the Spirit.

[60] We have a picture of "cleaning up" in the Old Testament preparations for the Passover. It was to be a time of spiritual preparation and examination, a time to clean house — what we would now call a spiritual spring-cleaning. Read about it in Exodus 12:15 & 13:7. It was during this time the Israelites cleansed their cooking utensils and cleansed their homes of all chametz or leaven. This practice was given to them as a picture of the necessity of cleaning all sin and rebellion from every nook and cranny of their lives. Even today, practicing Jews clean chametz from their homes, refrigerators, cars, offices, clothing, and everything that touches their daily lives. We too are called to cleanse "chametz" from our lives continually and not just once a year. See 1 Corinthians 5:8.

"I adorned you with jewelry: I put bracelets on your arms and a necklace around your neck, and I put a ring on your nose, earrings on your ears and a beautiful crown on your head. So you were adorned with gold and silver; your clothes were of fine linen and costly fabric and embroidered cloth."
(Ezekiel 16:11)

Our Lord Jesus Christ makes His bride beautiful with His spiritual treasures. And He desires for all of us to be adorned, ready for the day of His return.

The disciples gathered with a purpose on the day of Pentecost (Acts chapter 2). It wasn't a prayer meeting to ask for spiritual gifts; they were waiting for "the Gift." They were all together in one place, as Jesus had commanded them. They gathered in obedience to Jesus' words, "Do not leave Jerusalem, but wait for the gift my Father promised, which you have heard me speak about. For John baptized with water, but in a few days you will be baptized with the Holy Spirit" (Acts 1:4-5). They gathered in reverent awe before the Lord, and they received power when the Holy Spirit came upon them to make them witnesses in their home town of Jerusalem, in their region of Judea, to their neighbors in Samaria, and to the ends of the earth.

Again, it must be clear. There is no formula, no ten steps to receiving the spiritual gift of prophecy or any of the gifts of the Spirit. No amount of repentance fully prepares us, even though we ought to continually come before God with a contrite heart. We come before the Lord in obedience and reverent awe, worshipping, exalting, and honoring our mighty and awesome God. We come before God knowing that it is the will and desire of our Lord Jesus to give good gifts to adorn His bride for the good of His church and His eternal kingdom.[61]

---

[61] Some denominations teach that the gifts of the Spirit are given when a believer is baptized with water. Others teach that the gifts are given when a believer is baptized in the Holy Spirit, and always with the evidence of speaking with tongues. My belief is that God will give gifts to whom He chooses and at the time of His choosing and not necessarily at a specific time or in a specific way. Just for discussion's sake, let's say that God chooses to impart spiritual gifts to a convert when he or she is baptized in water. Even so, the spiritual gift must be empowered in the believer, and a most excellent way is by the laying on of hands by the elders, pastor, or presbyter.

Keep in mind, it is good for us to be content in the ministries and office we have, in the opportunities to serve we find in front of us — this is important: "For I have learned to be content whatever the circumstances" (Philippians 4:11). Be content, live in gratitude, bloom where you're planted and be faithful in the gift you have. When you desire this gift, as the Apostle Paul encouraged, ask, knowing that it is God's will to give His good gifts to the bride of Christ.

A word of caution: When we focus on others, their gifts and offices, we are in danger of wallowing in destructive envy. In fear, we hide this all too common sin of envy, often hiding it and allowing poisonous venom to flow out in indirect, sometimes subtly vicious ways. Coveting others' gifts is a sickness of the soul, destructive to fellowship and too often a sin we tend to keep secret, destroying the church from within like a cancer.

Jesus' command to "wait" is still critical to our understanding of receiving spiritual gifts in the church today. We must not be quick to send Christians into service in the church until they are ready with gifts empowered by the Holy Spirit. As the Lord told Zerubbabel, "This is the word of the Lord to Zerubbabel: 'Not by might nor by power, but by my Spirit,' says the Lord Almighty. 'What are you, O mighty mountain? Before Zerubbabel you will become level ground'" (Zechariah 4:6). We cannot move mountains apart from faith and the power of the Holy Spirit working through us (Matthew 17:20). Obstacles that stand in the way of the advancing kingdom of God cannot be moved with human might, a man's words, or personal strength. When we dig into the original Hebrew in Zechariah 4:6, we see that it is clearly saying, "Not by the strength of man. Not by temporal power."

It is also good to understand this waiting to which we are called. It can't be an inactive, sitting on the couch, remote in hand kind of waiting. "But those who wait on the Lord will find new strength. They will fly high on wings like eagles. They will run and not grow weary. They will walk and not faint" (Isaiah 40:31). The Hebrew word for "wait" קָוָה (kävä') has the connotation of adhering to, binding ourselves to, as being tied together. Any other kind of waiting can lead to despair, bitterness, and pessimism.

We must wait, adhere to, bind ourselves to our Lord God and be empowered for the ministries of our Lord in His church and His eternal kingdom. It is good to wait for the power of the Spirit so that we may effectively become witnesses and go to our neighbors and our community, upholding the Good News Gospel of Jesus Christ to a lost and dying world.

E. Continue being filled

Receiving the gifting and empowering work of the Holy Spirit is not a one-time, once-for-all-time experience. Ephesians 5:18 reminds us, "Instead, be filled with the Holy Spirit."[62] God is a God who continually molds, reshapes, and refreshes us. We need His fountain of blessing to continually flow from deep within us and through us as we minister in the gifts to which we are called.

The moment of justification is the beginning of God's work of saving grace in our lives, and is the moment we receive the Holy Spirit. Christians are saved (justified), being saved (sanctified) and living in expectation of eternal salvation (glorified). Yet God has even more blessings for us: the empowering work of the Holy Spirit and the gifting of the Holy Spirit. This baptism by fire is the beginning of a Spirit-empowered Christian life of service and ministry, just as justification starts us on a pathway called sanctification. We do not get a Holy-Spirit-anointing-and-you're-good-to-go-until-you're-toes-up-or-until-Jesus-returns. We must press on. "Keep on being filled with the Spirit" (Ephesians 5:18b ISV). "And the disciples were continually filled with joy and with the Holy Spirit" (Acts 13:52 NASB).

To receive the gifting and empowering work of the Spirit of Jesus and the gift He has ordained for you, simply ask. Earnestly pray and

---

[62] Source: *Systematic Theology* by Dr. Wayne Grudem, pg 781. On Ephesians 5:18: "He uses a present tense imperative verb that could more explicitly be translated, 'Be continually being filled with the Holy Spirit,' thus implying that this is something that should repeatedly be happening to Christians. Such fullness of the Holy Spirit will result in renewed worship and thanksgiving (Eph. 5:18-20), and in renewed relationships to others, especially those in authority over us or those under our authority (Eph. 5:21-6:9)."

ask your Heavenly Father for what you desire. He put the desire in your heart and will be faithful to accomplish the good work He began in you. The work is difficult. There will be hazards at every turn, but you must not toss aside the Bridegroom's precious treasures, because the good work you will accomplish is of great benefit to all who you will touch. Be encouraged to continually come to the fountain of blessing to immerse yourself and saturate your whole being in the blessed flow. Remain in God's council, by the power of God's Word and the work of the Holy Spirit, and continually receive from the Precious Flow. And keep on being filled.

Our Prayer:

> *Oh Lord God Almighty,*
> *Creator of all heaven and earth,*
> *Forgive us for rejecting the good gifts You hold out to Your bride to beautifully adorn Your church for the glory of Your Holy Name. Give us hearts that desire to worship You in reverence and awe, for You are the Giver of precious gifts for Your bride, given to us by Your grace and at such great cost — given for the good of Your church. Open our hearts to receive all You desire for us to empower us to serve in Your church and Your kingdom. Open our understanding to know You, to know Your goodness, Your grace, and Your mercy so evident in this great spiritual gift of prophecy.*
> *For the sake of the Holy Name of Jesus, Who is the Great Amen.*

Your Journey Journal

Q & A Chapter 3
Christ's Word Present in Prophecy

A.   Why is it important to ask for the spiritual gift of prophecy?

B.   Have you counted the cost of serving in this spiritual gift?

C.   What are the benefits of the ministries of this spiritual gift?

Your Journal Notes:

4

Serving Together Strengthens the Gift

Loner, maverick, rugged individualist, and loose cannon are terms that should not be needed to describe those who minister and serve in the gifts of the Holy Spirit. Strike these characteristics from your thinking and remove them from your vocabulary, because these traits are destructive, divisive, and incompatible with spiritual gifts. In true ministries of the spiritual gifts, words that divide are replaced with healing words like unity, together, building up, strengthening, encouragement, and agreement.

For the purpose of unity, godly leadership will help the ministries and service of spiritual gifts to be most effective in fulfilling the call of the Great Commission. We turn to Jesus, the Head of the church, and to the Holy Spirit sent by Jesus to bring us together. We work shoulder-to-shoulder with Christ Jesus and our brothers and sisters in the Lord to accomplish all God commands us to do. Together with Christ Jesus, godly leaders, and those who serve with us, we are strengthened to serve.

> *"So Christ himself gave the apostles, the prophets, the evangelists, the pastors and teachers, to equip his people for works of service, so that the body of Christ may be built up until we all reach unity in the faith and in the knowledge of the Son of God and become mature, attaining to the whole measure of the fullness of Christ." (Ephesians 4:11-13)*

A: Prophecy works with other spiritual gifts

We must hear the Apostle Paul's appeal as we bring this teaching on spiritual gifts to a conclusion: "Now eagerly desire the greater gifts" (1 Corinthians 12:31). He makes perfectly clear in chapter 14 which of the spiritual gifts is the greater: "Follow the way of love and eagerly desire gifts of the Spirit, especially prophecy" (1 Corinthians 14:1). Beyond a doubt, this spiritual gift is of great importance in the church today; it is most beneficial, and it is a gift that reveals the heart of God to His people as they come together to worship. And God calls us to serve within His established order so that spiritual gifts are effectively ministered. Godly order is like clockworks that mesh together to keep time and is best accomplished by means of purposeful leadership and the spiritual gift of presbytery.

But you can't understand the two verses above in 1 Corinthians 12 and 14 without considering what Paul writes in the rest of chapter 12. In this part of his letter to the church he uses the analogy of the human body to illustrate that the church has many working parts, and the importance of all of them:

> "Just as a body, though one, has many parts, but all its many parts form one body, so it is with Christ. For we were all baptized by one Spirit so as to form one body — whether Jews or Gentiles, slave or free — and we were all given the one Spirit to drink. Even so the body is not made up of one part but of many.
>
> Now if the foot should say, 'Because I am not a hand, I do not belong to the body,' it would not for that reason stop being part of the body. And if the ear should say, 'Because I am not an eye, I do not belong to the body,' it would not for that reason stop being part of the body. If the whole body were an eye, where would the sense of hearing be? If the whole body were an ear, where would the sense of smell be? But in fact God has placed the parts in the body, every one of them, just as he wanted them to be. If they were all one

part, where would the body be? As it is, there are many parts, but one body.

The eye cannot say to the hand, 'I don't need you!' And the head cannot say to the feet, 'I don't need you!' On the contrary, those parts of the body that seem to be weaker are indispensable, and the parts that we think are less honorable we treat with special honor. And the parts that are unpresentable are treated with special modesty, while our presentable parts need no special treatment. But God has put the body together, giving greater honor to the parts that lacked it, so that there should be no division in the body, but that its parts should have equal concern for each other. If one part suffers, every part suffers with it; if one part is honored, every part rejoices with it." (1 Corinthians 12:1-26)

Remember — should the Holy Spirit desire to gift you with the spiritual gift of prophecy, one of the most desirable and useful of the gifts, this does not elevate you above all those who minister in other gifts. This gift is greater because it is more beneficial, not because it elevates the prophet to a higher spiritual status in the church. This gift does not put you on a pedestal and it does not make you more spiritual.

B. Team work

In today's American culture we may better understand the principle of one body with many working parts by using a sports analogy. The ministries of spiritual gifts are like a team sport. You cannot mount an offense and you can't have an effective defense if you are playing on an all-star team of one. If the quarterback thinks, "I don't need the rest of the team," his pride sets himself up for a fall (Proverbs 16:18).

A football team consists of many specific positions and none of them serves a greater purpose than the others. Typically, how many touchdowns does the quarterback make? None. Often, the highest scorer is the kicker who chalks up those three pointers; but how many passes does he catch? None. The three hundred pound center snaps the ball on queue and blocks his man, but how many passes does he throw? None. It takes a team that includes everyone, even the water boy. We must not belittle any of the spiritual gifts or those who minister in them because they are all necessary and must work together. When a spiritual gift is missing from the church, just like when the linebacker doesn't line up — the whole team suffers.

A healthy, effective church requires all the gifts of the Spirit to be operating in the service and ministries of the church. As a part of my personal study on this topic, I listed the number of gifted and empowered people necessary to have a fully functioning church team (body). The tally came up to fifty, including more than one person to minister in some spiritual gifts. Conclusion? To fill all the offices of the church with all spiritual gifts fully functioning, approximately fifty men and women are necessary to complete the "team." (Spiritually gifted and empowered teens may be included as the Spirit wills.)

Creating a complete team does not happen by osmosis or by accident. The church doesn't accidently evolve into an effective team. A team comes together by purposeful, prayerful guidance, and leadership. The effective ministries of the church happen by means of godly leaders who depend upon the leading of the Holy Spirit, who gives spiritual gifts as He desires. "All these [gifts] are the work of one and the same Spirit, and he distributes them to each one, just as he determines" (1 Corinthians 12:11).

What would a church look like if everyone ministered in the spiritual gift of prophecy? What kind of gathering would you have if everyone served in the gift of administration and no one had the spiritual gift of generosity? God provides the gift of leadership for the church for the purpose of managing the effective ministries of spiritual gifts. Leaders will make sure that each local team of believers has all the positions filled with people who are fully prepared to serve. The person operating in this gift in the local church is called a Presbyter. In the Scriptures, we see this gift in operation: "Neglect not the gift that is in thee, which was given thee by prophecy, with the laying on of the hands of the presbytery" (1 Timothy 4:14 ASV).

C. Leading the team

This ministry gift of leadership will provide the means for a church to fully function in the effective ministries of all the gifts of the Spirit. Also, for the spiritual gift of prophecy to be most powerfully ministered, godly order provided by leaders in the church is necessary. Godly leadership does not stifle the gifts, but strengthens those who are gifted by the Spirit.

The presbyter and other leaders will seek to know the desire of the Holy Spirit through prayer and fasting. Then he or she will impart spiritual gifts as the Spirit desires by laying hands on the person, declaring the Spirit's anointing; this event is often accompanied with prophecies to confirm the gift. The presbyter will mentor, teach, train, encourage, build up, admonish, discipline, and oversee the ministries and services of spiritual gifts in the church, according to the guiding truths of Scripture and the direction of the Holy Spirit of Jesus.

Now, with the presbyter providing a godly order for the ministries and service of spiritual gifts, the gift to be most desired, the spiritual gift of prophecy, can be beautifully ministered as a part of the whole — as a functioning member of the team, to accomplish all that God has purposed and planned in giving the beautiful adornments He has provided for the church. Now, gifted, equipped, and empowered, the team will accomplish what Christ Jesus compelled us to do as His church.

Jesus, who is Captain of the "team," has called the play, the team is in formation at the line of scrimmage, and now we can see how the various gifts work together. The gift of presbytery and the spiritual gift of prophecy will often function with one purpose. The presbyter fasts, prays, and lays hands to impart and empower a spiritual gift to a disciple of Christ and then the prophet confirms the gift as he or she receives affirmation from the Spirit.

In the same way, those who are gifted with the spiritual gift of words of knowledge or words of wisdom work hand in hand with healing gifts by speaking out God's word in the moment. As the word of knowledge or wisdom is heard, faith to be healed is given to the one in need of healing.

The spiritual gift of healing may work together with the spiritual gift of prophecy. The person gifted to extend Jesus' healing touch lays hands on the sick person and the one gifted in prophecy will confirm God's healing touch.[63] Preaching from the pulpit can work together with the spiritual gift of prophecy as the prophet proclaims by spontaneous anointing, confirming the message by saying, in effect: "It's important to pay attention to what you just heard from the pulpit."

The spiritual gift of singing a spiritual song, a new song, works hand in glove with the spiritual gift of prophecy. In fact, singing in the Spirit is a form of prophetic utterance. The picture that comes to mind is that of a singer and prophet proclaiming God's message like they are double-teaming. One might sing the melody and another the words. But be flexible because there is no formula that must be followed.

Those who minister in the spiritual gift of discerning of spirits are necessary when examining a prophetic message offered in the church gathering, teaming with other congregants. This spiritual gift is very effective for the purpose of determining the source of a message; is it genuinely based in God's Word or did it come from human reasoning or some other source? And this is a team effort.

Please be clear in your understanding of this concept of spiritual gifts working together in teamwork. There are few instances where spiritual gifts are ministered in isolation, without a strengthening and supportive team of whom Christ is the Head. The ministries and service of spiritual gifts are intended to work together, as a squad, to accomplish Christ's Great Commission to go forth to family, neighborhoods, communities, cities, states, nations, and to all the world to preach Christ, His atoning death, and the power of the resurrection, making disciples and baptizing them in the Name of the Father and in the Name of the Son and in Name of the Holy Spirit.

---

[63] It is quite common for a person who is healed to begin to slip into doubt when the pain memories come back, or some other symptom is brought back in a subconscious memory. Confirmation of a healing by means of prophetic ministry will bolster a person's faith to hold fast in their restored healthy state.

D. Better together

Find a team of Christians who are like-minded and who will encourage you to grow in grace and knowledge, who will strengthen you in the ministries and services of spiritual gifts. Be encouraged to desire the greatest gift to minister the greatest good. Ask your Lord Jesus for the gift you desire and then serve in the gift, faith, and power you have received for the good of the whole team.

The spiritual gift of prophecy is the most desirable and effective in building up the church and the Holy Spirit will give the gift to those He desires. The Spirit of Jesus will gift you and empower you for ministry and service for the good of all those who will minister shoulder to shoulder with you. This is what He has promised. This is what He will do.

E. Jesus, the Giver of Gifts

"Every good and perfect gift is from above, coming down from the Father of the heavenly lights, who does not change like shifting shadows" (James 1:17). This is His name, Giver of Gifts. When the church began, on its first day, precious, empowering gifts were given to those who gathered together to pray. God has not changed. He is not a shifting shadow. His precious gifts are held out to those who ask even today. Ask the Giver of Gifts and then wait upon Him. You will receive His good gifts.

"If you love me, you will keep my commandments" (John 14:15 ESV). Because of our overwhelming love for our Lord Jesus Christ, and by the gifting and empowering work of the Spirit, we will fulfill His commandment to the church to go into all the world with His message of saving grace. "And I will ask the Father, and he will give you another Helper, to be with you forever, even the Spirit of truth, whom the world cannot receive, because it neither sees him nor knows him. You know him, for he dwells with you and will be in you" (John 14:16-17 ESV).

Will you be like the maverick riding toward the horizon, a loner on a mission? Or will you take this message of saving grace to a lost and dying world, standing shoulder to shoulder with your brothers and sisters in the Lord? Will you minister like the rugged individualist who strikes out on his or her own or will you join arms with fellow Christians to be strong together, in the power of His might? With words of great wisdom, Solomon wrote: "Though one may be overpowered, two can defend themselves. A cord of three strands is not quickly broken" (Ecclesiastes 4:12). We are better, stronger, and much safer as we minister and serve in the strength of Christian community, by the anointing and power of the Holy Spirit.

Your Journey Journal

Q & A Chapter 4
Serving Together Strengthens the Gift

A.   Describe how spiritual gifts work together. Give an example.

B.   What is the role of church leadership in the ministries of spiritual gifts?

C.   Why are mavericks ineffective in ministries of spiritual gifts?

Your Journal Notes:

Going Forward

The Call is Clear

The lion has roared —
who will not fear?
The Sovereign Lord has spoken —
who can but prophesy?
Amos 3:8

The Holy Spirit proceeds from the Father and from the Son with precious and power-filled gifts for the church, to adorn His bride in preparation for His return. "I saw the Holy City, the new Jerusalem, coming down out of heaven from God, prepared as a bride beautifully dressed for her husband" (Revelation 21:2).

To prepare you for the great wedding feast, the Bridegroom sends good gifts to you to adorn you with heaven's ornaments — gold and precious stones. With these good gifts, heaven's treasures are revealed to you. God's perfect will, purpose, and plan is for these precious gifts — heaven's family treasures, to be displayed in great splendor so that His name may be glorified in all the earth. As we receive and cherish these gifts, our hearts become centered upon what is of eternal value.

> *"Do not be afraid, little flock, for your Father has been pleased to give you the kingdom. Sell your possessions and give to the poor. Provide purses for yourselves that will not wear out, a treasure in heaven that will never fail, where no thief comes near and no moth destroys. For where your treasure is, there your heart will be also." (Luke 12:32-34)*

Is your heart in heaven? Will you receive His good gifts? Will you treasure His good gifts in the same way He treasures you (Matthew

13:45)? How precious are the Jewels of the kingdom of heaven? The New Jerusalem descends as a bride adorned with precious ornaments for her wedding: "I saw the Holy City, the new Jerusalem, coming down out of heaven from God, prepared as a bride beautifully dressed for her husband" (Revelation 21:2).

Precious stones are the foundation of the New Jerusalem. The bride of Christ is adorned with beautiful and precious jewels. Say "yes" to all that our Christ Jesus holds out to you, and you will be arrayed as a bride for His coming. Earnestly pray. Fervently pray. "The prayer of a righteous person is powerful and effective" (James 5:16). Knock and keep knocking until the door is opened to you. "Ask and it will be given to you; seek and you will find; knock and the door will be opened to you. For everyone who asks receives; the one who seeks finds; and to the one who knocks, the door will be opened" (Matthew 7:7-8). And especially seek the most beneficial gift of the Spirit, a precious jewel of the kingdom, the spiritual gift of prophecy.

What is at stake here is the temporal versus the eternal. This truth is crucial for those who minister and serve in spiritual gifts rather than in our God-given natural gifts alone. As the apostle Paul wraps up 1 Corinthians, he states clearly: "I declare to you, brothers and sisters, that flesh and blood cannot inherit the kingdom of God, nor does the perishable inherit the imperishable" (1 Corinthians 15:50). Paul makes a clear demarcation between temporal and eternal, perishable and imperishable, and mortal and immortal. What is eternal, what is imperishable, and what is immortal is what will stand the test of fire — the precious jewels of the kingdom of heaven.

Paul concludes with a "Therefore" that is wonderfully informative: "Therefore, my dear brothers and sisters, stand firm. Let nothing move you. Always give yourselves fully to the work of the Lord, because you know that your labor in the Lord is not in vain" (1 Corinthians 15:58). Your labor in the Lord is not in vain because your ministry and service as the church is accomplished "'not by might nor by power, but by my Spirit,' says the Lord Almighty" (Zechariah 4:6). Your work, your service, and your ministry as your part in the church body begins now. All that you do in Christ and the Spirit prepares you as a bride for the Bridegroom's return. Your work will be completed in the power of the Spirit and strengthen the church community with eternal effect. Beyond a doubt, through the work for which the Holy Spirit has gifted and empowered you, you can change eternity for many lost souls.

The desire of God's heart today is to gift and empower His people as the Spirit chooses to strengthen His church by means of spiritual gifts. The greatest and most desirable of these gifts is the spiritual gift of prophecy.

Now is the time to respond to Jesus' call and say, "Yes, Lord. Amen. All for the glory and honor of Your Holy Name."

"Then he said to me,
"Prophesy to these bones and say to them,
'Dry bones, hear the word of the Lord!"
Ezekiel 37:4

Appendix

Recommended resources for study and reading:

Every serious student of Scripture would do well to make time for earnest prayer, seeking the Lord, interceding for the church and our shepherds. It is also beneficial acquire the following study resources, as your budget allows:

1) The Holy Bible in reliable versions (NIV, NLT, ESV, NRSV)
2) Personal notebook or journal
3) Topical Bible: *The Zondervan NIV Nave's Topical Bible.*
4) A written systematic theology: *Systematic Theology* by Wayne Grudem
5) *Book of Concord*, Translated by Theodore G. Tappert.
6) Bible Dictionary: *Vine's Expository Dictionary*, by W.E. Vine.
7) Concordance: *Strong's Exhaustive Concordance of the Bible*, by James Strong.
8) Bible commentary: *Matthew Henry's Commentary:* and *Jamieson, Fausset and Brown Commentary.*

Many of these resources are available online (www.blueletterbible.org and www.bible.cc/).

Additional reading:
The Beauty of Spiritual Language by Jack Hayford
Authority to Heal by Ken Blue
The Spiritual Man by Watchman Nee
The Pursuit of God by A. W. Tozer

Notes, Quotes & Credits

Pg 37. *Preaching for the Church* by R. R. Caemmerer. © 1959. Concordia Publishing House, St. Louis, Missouri. Used by permission.

Pg 38. *A Study in the History of the Eucharist* by J. T. Shotwell. Doctoral Thesis, Eyre and Spottingswoode, London.

Pg 42. *God Uses Cracked Pots* by Patsy Clairmont. © 1991. Thomas Nelson, Publisher.

Pg 47. *Authority to Heal* by Ken Blue. © 1987 Ken Blue. InterVarsity Press, PO Box 1400, Downers Grove, IL 60515. Used by permission.

Pg 50. *Preaching for the Church* by R.R. Caemmerer. © 1959. Concordia Publishing House, St. Louis, Missouri. Used by permission.

Pg 59. John Calvin, as quoted in *The Gift of Prophecy in 1 Corinthians* by Wayne A. Grudem. © 1999. Wipf and Stock Publishers. Used by permission.

Pg 61. *Spirit Rising: Tapping into the Power of the Holy Spirit* by Jim Cymbala. © 2012. Used by permission of Zondervan Publishing.

Pg 67. *Women of the Bible* by Ann Spangler and Jean E. Syswerda. pg 423. © 1999. Zondervan Publishing House, Grand Rapids, MI 49530.

Pg 93. *Systematic Theology* by Wayne Grudem. © 1994. Inter-Varsity Press and Zondervan, Grand Rapids, MI.

Glossary

The purpose of this glossary is not to repeat definitions available in a Bible Dictionary, but to offer dimensions of the original words and relate how these meanings apply to the study of *Treasures of the Kingdom*. Also listed are terms used in this study that are not in common use today.

- **Adorned, Adornments,** עָדָה (*'adah*), κοσμέω (*kosmeō*): The bride of Christ is given bridal adornments, or ornaments of worship for the glory and honor of the Bridegroom. These are not only for the time when the Bridegroom returns for His bride, but for the age of the church — the bride in waiting. Ezekiel beautifully creates a complete picture of this word, showing the blight washed away and beauty given in its place (Ezekiel 15:11-13). Revelation 21:2 reveals another dimension, "as a bride adorned for her husband."

- **Authority, Authority of the Believer,** ἐξουσία (*exousia*): God is Authority. His Name is Authority. Christ's position at the right hand of the Father is Authority. Christ Jesus confers His authority on whomever he pleases. For the believer, submission is the key to all authority. Christians have *NO* authority apart from Christ, the Head of the church, and what He commands us to do. All authority in Christ comes by virtue of our submission to His authority and the Word. God has established an order of authority for the church and for the family. This authority has a heart of love, the heart of a servant, a foot-washing mindset. As an example: Jesus had authority to lay His life down because of His reverent submission to the Authority of His Father.

- **Body of Man, Natural,** σῶμα (*sōma*): Scripture refers to our earthly body as earthen vessels, jars of clay, perishable, a tent, or a house. In this study it is, at times, referred to as our earth suit. We can't mistake what it is. We can pinch it, poke it, walk about in it, feel pain, experience pleasure, laugh, shed tears, break a bone, and the list goes on. This body is our means for remaining here on earth to accomplish all that God has ordained for us to do.

- **Cessation, Cessationist:** Those within the Christian church who believe that many of the spiritual gifts have ceased, especially utterance gifts, are considered to be cessationists. Their belief system is promoted in many different ways. Some don't outright deny prophecy, but instead redefine it as preaching — pulpit ministry. Others simply overlook these spiritual gifts and refuse to acknowledge them or teach truthfully about them. Still others claim that these gifts were only needed for the establishment of the church in the beginning of the church age. Still others teach that God only speaks to His people today in the written, canonical Scripture. In addition, some claim that spiritual gifts are nothing more than God-given natural gifts, applied for spiritual purposes within the church.

- **Church, ἐκκλησία (ekklēsia):** The universal body of all Christian believers who are called by Jesus' Name and gather together in Jesus' Name. The church is Christ. It is the means by which Christ is manifested to a lost and dying world. A church gathering will consist of three parts: Christ, the Head; Leaders (under authority) who establish order, i.e. pastors, elders, deacons, deaconesses, etc.; and congregants (under authority) who also minister and serve in the church. It is a gathering for worship, for serving, for singing praises before the Lord, and for the preparation of the saints to minister the saving grace of our Lord and Savior, Jesus Christ. To be a church, order must be established; an order of authority, just as there is order in God's created universe. Note: This is not one person in authority, but an order of authority (1 Corinthians 14:40).

- **Commission, οἰκονομία (oikonomia):** The Great Commission of the Christian Church came through a command from our Lord Jesus. He instructed his disciples, then and throughout the age of the church, to make disciples, baptize them, and teach them to obey, revealing and ministering the resurrected, living Jesus Christ to every tribe, nation, people, and tongue in all the earth (Matthew 28:18-20). A church, in submission to Christ, may, under the authority of the Great Commission, appoint one of their people to a specific calling, duty, ministry, or mission through fasting, prayer, and the laying on of hands.

- **Common Grace:** This refers to the grace of God that is common to all mankind. The benefits of God's common grace are for all humans for the purpose of giving them the means to earn their way and to provide for their families. These common gifts and talents are for the good of societies and cultures, "for he makes his sun rise on the evil and on the good, and sends rain on the righteous and on the unrighteous" (Matthew 5:45 NRSV).

- **Covenant** ברית (*berith*), διαθηκη (*diatheke*): God made a covenant with Abram, Noah, King David and many more. God is a God of covenants. This is His very nature. In His covenants with people, He promises His goodness and His blessings, each revealing and fulfilling His purpose and plan for all eternity. God's covenants are one-sided grants, and at times give conditions (if you ..., then I ...) and establish requirements as in the Mosaic covenant and in His covenant with King David: "*if* your sons keep my covenant and the statutes I teach them, *then* their sons will sit on your throne forever and ever" (Psalm 132:12, emphasis added). As New Testament Christians, we have a covenant sealed by the blood of a risen Savior who has satisfied the "If you" requirements of the covenant.

- **Covenant, Sign of:** God gave "signs" along with His covenants. To Abram He gave a new name (Abraham), to Noah he gave a rainbow, to King David a kingdom and lineage eternally blessed. Jesus is the Mediator of a covenant for the New Testament church, and He gives a sign: His Holy Spirit. He confirmed this covenant and gives all who are His disciples His robe of righteousness.

- **Empowering of Spiritual Gifts:** From ages past God has ordained for **_all_** who are called by His Name, a work, service, or ministry (Ephesians 2:10). For this work, God gifts His people to accomplish what He has called them to do. Whether these gifts are given when a soul receives the gift of saving faith or in a subsequent outpouring of the Spirit of Grace, these spiritual gifts must be empowered by the Holy Spirit. Apart from an empowering work of the Spirit and without continual, ongoing, refreshing anointing from the Holy Spirit, these gifts are like a sailing ship with no wind, or a lamp without oil, or a car without fuel.

- **Ecstatic Experience:** There are many examples of ecstatic experiences throughout Scripture. Abram's is recorded in Genesis 15:12: "As the sun was setting, Abram fell into a deep sleep, and a thick and dreadful darkness came over him." Ezekiel says in Ezekiel 1:1, "the heavens were opened and I saw visions of God." The Apostle Paul was "caught up into the third heaven" (2 Corinthians 12:2). John the Apostle writes in Revelation 1:10, "On the Lord's Day I was in the Spirit, and I heard behind me a loud voice like a trumpet." Ministries within the church in a spiritual gift, whether prophecies, spiritual languages and interpretations, or singing in the spirit, typically do not involve any kind of ecstatic experience. Ecstatic experiences as listed above are uncommon in everyday Christian life. Yet they must not be relegated to a time long past.

- **Fallibility:** The word "fallible" is not found in Scripture. But we find similar words that make its meaning clear: Fall, Fallen, Falling and Fell. In essence, we ought to always keep in mind that we are all fallible, i.e. subject to false steps, blunders, trespasses, moral failings, offenses, lapses of judgment, and the list goes on. Often it's a daily process of acknowledging our weaknesses, praying for strength to overcome them and then confessing our failings to receive forgiveness of our sin and God's cleansing flow.

- **Filled with the Spirit,** πίμπλημι (*pimplēmi*): Some would refer to this as the Baptism of the Holy Spirit. Others believe that we receive all that the Holy Spirit has for us as we come to saving faith. The controversies are not worth the trouble. In searching Scripture, this is what I see: When saving faith is given to a soul, the Holy Spirit indwells them. The Spirit of God washes over them and through them, cleansing them and sealing them against God's just wrath. The believer is "born of the Spirit." But the Holy Spirit isn't finished in His ministries to the new disciple. This adopted child must continually be filled and refilled in the Holy Spirit. There are also subsequent, powerful infillings or empowering of the Holy Spirit when the spiritual gifts are empowered for the good of the whole church, for deeds of service, worship, and ministry to the body of believers. The Old and New Testaments reveal a clear demarcation in the ministries of the Holy Spirit. In the Old, the Holy Spirit washes over or comes upon people, and in the New, the Holy Spirit indwells His people, filling them from within like springs of Living Water.

- **Foretell:** To foretell is to tell something which cannot be known by natural means, intuition, investigation, scientific methods, or through any other human enterprise, especially to predict events before they occur. Foretelling prophecies are centered on the coming Messiah, focused upon Jesus Christ. These future events are known only to the mind of God and are made known to whom God chooses by the revelation power of the Holy Spirit.

- **Forthtell:** To deliver a message from God, whether with reference to the past, the present, or future. This ministry in the church is speaking forth the mind and counsel of God through prophetic utterance. Through "forthtelling," Jesus Christ is revealed by revelation power of the Holy Spirit. In this prophetic ministry there will be godly counsel, correction, admonition, exposed sins, encouragement, enlightenment, direction, and building up of the saints. Prophetic messages for the purpose of forthtelling proclaim a clear, specific, and authoritative message. They are not expressed in broad and general terms that are subject to various interpretations.

- **Infallibility:** Incapable of failing or failure, unerring in doctrine. Old Testament prophets were held to a standard of infallibility. Should they utter a prophetic message, whether foretelling or forthtelling, the message must prove true or they were marked as false prophets. Those who minister in the spiritual gift of prophecy are not held to this standard of infallibility for the words they choose to express the message they offer. But they must submit to the gathering of believers and church leaders for examination of the content of their messages, using Scripture as the standard.

- **Kingdom of Heaven/God:** The church is not the Kingdom of God, but is a part of God's Kingdom. The Kingdom of God is principally the sovereign rule of God (where God's will is done), manifested in Christ to bring all things to be subject to Him (under His feet). Thus, the Kingdom of God is the reign of God, and the church is a community or fellowship given to God's people within the Kingdom. These Scriptures are key to our understanding: Mark 9:1, Matthew 3:2, 4:17, 10:7, Luke 21:31. Note: Jesus and His disciples preached, taught, and healed, as they proclaimed, "The Kingdom of Heaven has come near to you."

- **Spirit Filled,** πίμπλημι (*pimplēmi*): The term is not used specifically, but implied throughout this study. The study writer holds to the belief that the Holy Spirit indwells and seals those who are justified in Christ. Also, the Holy Spirit desires to work continuously in the lives of Christian disciples, gifting, empowering, refreshing, and anointing for works and ministries for the good of the church.

- **Spiritual Gifts,** χάρισμα (*charisma*): Gifts for ministries to the church, or within the church, given and empowered by the Holy Spirit are "spiritual gifts." In this study, we find it necessary to distinguish the common from the holy by separating the spiritual and natural gifts, even when those natural gifts are used for work and service in the church.